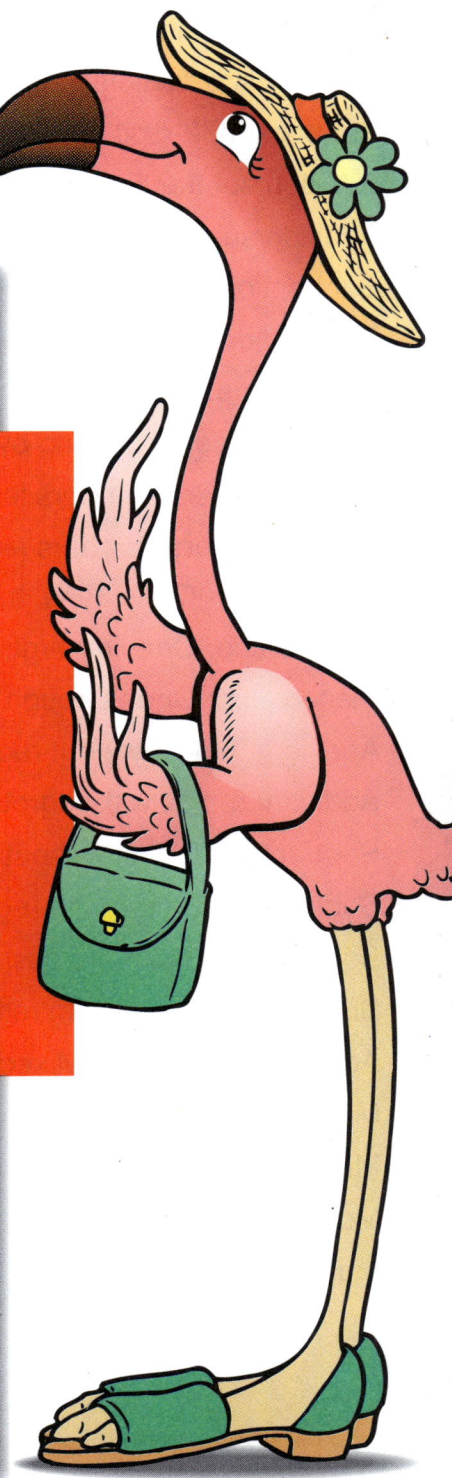

grade 3

The basic skills your 3rd grader needs!

- *Addition & Subtraction*
- *Time & Money*
- *Fractions*
- *Measurement*
- *Geometry*
- *Graphing*
- *Probability*
- *Problem Solving*
- *Multiplication & Division*
- *Patterns & Algebra*

Editor: Kathy Wolf
Contributing Writer: Amy Barsanti
Copy Editors: Tracy Johnson, Carol Rawleigh
Contributing Artist: Cathy Spangler Bruce
Typesetters: Lynette Dickerson, Mark Rainey
Cover Illustration and Design: Nick Greenwood

©2002 The Education Center, Inc.

Table of Contents

Numbers and Operations

Third-Grade Parent Pages 4
Addition: 2-digit, no regrouping 6
Addition: 2-digit with regrouping 7
Addition/subtraction 9
Subtraction: 2-digit with regrouping 10
Addition/subtraction 11
Addition/subtraction: Word problems 12
Subtraction: 3-digit with one regrouping 14
Subtraction: 3-digit with two regroupings 15
Place value: Expanded notation 19
Number order: Counting by 2s, 3s, 5s, 10s 20
Number order: Numbers less than 100 21
Number order: Numbers less than 1,000 22
Place value: Ones, tens, hundreds 23
Place value: Ones through thousands 25
Place value: Ones through 10,000s 26
Addition: 3-digit without regrouping 27
Addition: 3-digit with regrouping 28
Subtraction: 3-digit without regrouping 31
Subtraction: 3-digit with regrouping 32
Subtraction: 3-digit across zeros 33
Subtraction: 3-digit with regrouping 34
Addition/subtraction: Mixed practice 35
Multiplication: Table of facts 36
Multiplication: Introduction 37
Multiplication: Facts 0–5 38
Multiplication: Facts 6–7 39
Multiplication: Facts 7–9 40
Multiplication: Facts 5–9 41
Multiplication: Facts 1–9 42
Multiplication: Facts 10–12 43
Multiplication: Missing factors 44
Multiplication: Review 45
Division: Introduction 46
Division: Word problems 47

Fractions and Measurements

Third-Grade Parent Pages 48
Fractions: Parts of a whole 50
Fractions: Increasing a recipe 51
Fractions: Identifying fractional parts 52
Fractions: Parts of a group 53
Length: To nearest inch 55
Length: Distance in centimeters 56
Measurement: Perimeter in centimeters 57
Measurement: Perimeter 58
Measurement: Area in centimeters 59
Temperature: Comparing degrees C and F 60
Capacity: Cups, pints, quarts, gallons 61
Weight: Estimating pounds and ounces 62
Weight: Estimating metric units 63
Measurement review 64

©2002 by THE EDUCATION CENTER, INC.
All rights reserved.
ISBN# 1-56234-478-1

Except as provided for herein, no part of this publication may be reproduced or transmitted in any form or by any means, electronic or mechanical, including photocopying, recording, or storing in any information storage and retrieval system or electronic online bulletin board, without prior written permission from The Education Center, Inc. Permission is given to the original purchaser to reproduce patterns and reproducibles for individual and classroom use only and not for resale or distribution. Reproduction for an entire school or school system is prohibited. Please direct written inquiries to The Education Center, Inc., P.O. Box 9753, Greensboro, NC 27429-0753. The Education Center®, *Learning*®, and *Learning Library*® are registered trademarks of The Education Center, Inc. All other brand or product names are trademarks or registered trademarks of their respective companies.

Manufactured in the United States
10 9 8 7 6 5 4 3 2 1

Time and Money

Third-Grade Parent Page	65
Time to the quarter hour	66
Time to five minutes	68
Time: Word problems	69
Time to the minute	70
Time to five minutes	71
Time: Problem solving	72
Time: Elapsed time problems	73
Money: Counting coins	74
Money: Making change	75
Money: Adding amounts with decimals	76
Money: Addition/subtraction word problems	77

Geometry

Third-Grade Parent Pages	78
Polygons: Identifying triangles, quadrilaterals, hexagons, octagons, pentagons	80
Congruent figures	82
Lines, line segments, rays	83
Angles: Greater and less than a right angle	84
Symmetry	85
Transformations: Flips, slides, turns	86

Patterns, Functions, and Algebra

Third-Grade Parent Page	87
Patterns: Extending numbers and shapes	88
Patterns: Odd and even numbers	89
Functions: Find the rule	90
Functions: Missing factors	91
Algebra: Writing equations	92
Algebra: Writing equations, using calculator	93
Ordered pairs	94
Algebra word problems	96
Geometry, patterns, and algebra review	97

Graphing and Probability

Third-Grade Parent Page	99
Graphing: Reading a graph	100
Graphing: Completing a vertical bar graph	101
Graphing: Reading a horizontal bar graph	102
Graphing: Reading a line graph	103
Probability: Certain or impossible	104
Probability: Using a spinner	105
Probability: Least or most likely	106

Problem Solving

Third-Grade Parent Page	107
Working backward	108
Logical reasoning	109
Drawing a picture	110
Making a table	111
Finding a pattern	112
Making a list	113
Guessing and checking	114
Problem solving	115

Answer Keys 116

Third-Grade Parent Pages

Numbers and Operations

In third grade, numbers and operations are a big part of math instruction. This year your child develops his ability to deal with numbers mentally—to understand the relative size of numbers to 10,000 and to estimate the results of adding, subtracting, multiplying, and dividing. He develops his *number sense*.

Your child's biggest math task this year is to become fluent in addition and subtraction. He'll be solving problems with two- and three-digit numbers with *regrouping* of tens and hundreds. (You may have called this "borrowing" when you were in third grade.) Your child will also practice subtracting with borrowing across zeros. In the classroom, your child's teacher may have the students use manipulative sticks to reinforce place value of numbers with hundreds, tens, and ones. Your child will create and write numbers with *expanded notation* (237 = 200 + 30 + 7). Third graders will also add and subtract money amounts with decimals.

Your third grader already understands that repeated addition of equal sets is what multiplication is all about. He knows that division involves equal sharing or division of sets. He knows that the answer to a multiplication problem is called the *product* and that the two numbers being multiplied are called *factors*. Next comes the daunting task of committing the multiplication facts to memory—first facts to 5 and then 6 to 12.

Most third graders are both excited and challenged by this assignment. Plan time to listen to your child recite the facts over and over. Be supportive of his progress toward mastering one fact at a time. Learning the times table is a BIG DEAL! Let him know how proud you are of him!

This year, your third grader will learn to
- read and write numbers to ten thousands
- add and subtract two- and three-digit numbers with regrouping
- subtract across zeros
- find the missing factor in a multiplication problem
- multiply by one-digit numbers
- divide equal sets
- solve word problems using addition, subtraction, multiplication, and simple division

Key Math Skills for Grade 3
Numbers and Operations

- Counting, reading, and writing whole numbers to 10,000
- Addition: two-digit and three-digit with regrouping
- Subtraction: two-digit and three-digit with regrouping
- Subtraction: three-digit across zeros
- Addition and subtraction word problems: choosing the correct operation to solve a problem, identifying unnecessary information
- Multiplication: developing fluency with facts to 12
- Multiplication: finding missing factors
- Division: understanding the concept
- Number order: counting by 2s, 3s, 5s, and 10s
- Number order: ordering by tens, ones, and hundreds
- Place value: comparing numbers to 10,000 using <, >, =
- Place value: rounding to the nearest thousand
- Place value: expanded notation to 10,000 (for example: 1,362 = 1 thousand + 3 hundreds + 6 tens + 2 ones)

Numbers to 10,000
Help your child understand place value by discussing BIG numbers in everyday life. Together, read population signs on the roadways and compare thousands and ten thousands. Share and compare cash register receipts and discuss dollar amounts. Create addition and subtraction problems. How many more people live in your community than the one nearby? How much did you spend at the grocery store *AND* the video store?

Expanding On BIG Numbers
Third graders are proud to demonstrate their mastery of really BIG numbers. Ask your child to write the example above with expanded notation or to identify the digits in the tens, ones, hundreds, thousands, and ten thousands places. Challenge your gifted child to read and write state populations, newspaper circulation, or the number of burgers sold at McDonald's.

Name **K Aseh** Two-digit addition: No regrouping

Mouse on the Moon

Solve the problems.

A. 54 + 44 = 98

B. 73 + 13 = 86

C. 64 + 12 = 76

D. 44 + 50 = 94

E. 60 + 23 = 83

F. 39 + 40 = 79

G. 23 + 45 = 68

H. 17 + 60 = 77

I. 58 + 11 = 69

J. 22 + 37 = 59

K. 23 + 26 = 49

L. 60 + 32 = 92

M. 57 + 22 = 79

N. 31 + 27 = 58

O. 42 + 36 = 78

P. 25 + 53 = 78

Name_____   Addition: Two-digit with regrouping

Constellation Station

To add **2-digit numbers,** you may need to *regroup* the ones.
- First, add the ones.
- If the answer is more than 10, *regroup the ones.*

For example, the 11 ones are regrouped to make another group of ten and a group of 1.
- Next, write 1 above the tens place.
- Write the 1 in the ones place.
- Add all the tens.

Example:
```
  Tens
   1
   18
 + 33
 ----
    1
```

**Follow the steps.
Solve the problems.**

Example: 18 + 33 = 51
A. 68 + 27 = 95
B. 21 + 39 = 60
C. 15 + 55 = 70
D. 63 + 28 = 91
E. 29 + 14 = 43
F. 35 + 37 = 73
G. 12 + 79 = 91
H. 37 + 44 = 81
I. 36 + 25 = 61
J. 73 + 17 = 90
K. 36 + 28 = 64
L. 19 + 46 = 65
M. 69 + 29 = 98
N. 27 + 36 = 63
O. 46 + 16 = 62
P. 17 + 16 = 33

Try This: Connect the stars from 60 to 65 to find out Major Mouse's favorite constellation.

Name_____   Addition: Two-digit with regrouping

SMART COOKIE!

To add **2-digit numbers**, you may need to *regroup* the ones and tens.

Example:
```
  1
  18
+ 33
----
  51
```

A.
26
+ 27
53

B.
39
+ 58
97

C.
64
+ 18
82

D.
45
+ 16
01

E.
18
+ 52
60

F.
49
+ 34
83

G.
79
+ 3
82

H.
38
+ 54
92

I.
17
+ 59
76

At Home: Many restaurant fortune cookies have several "Lucky Numbers" listed on the fortune slip. Find the total sum of the numbers on yours.

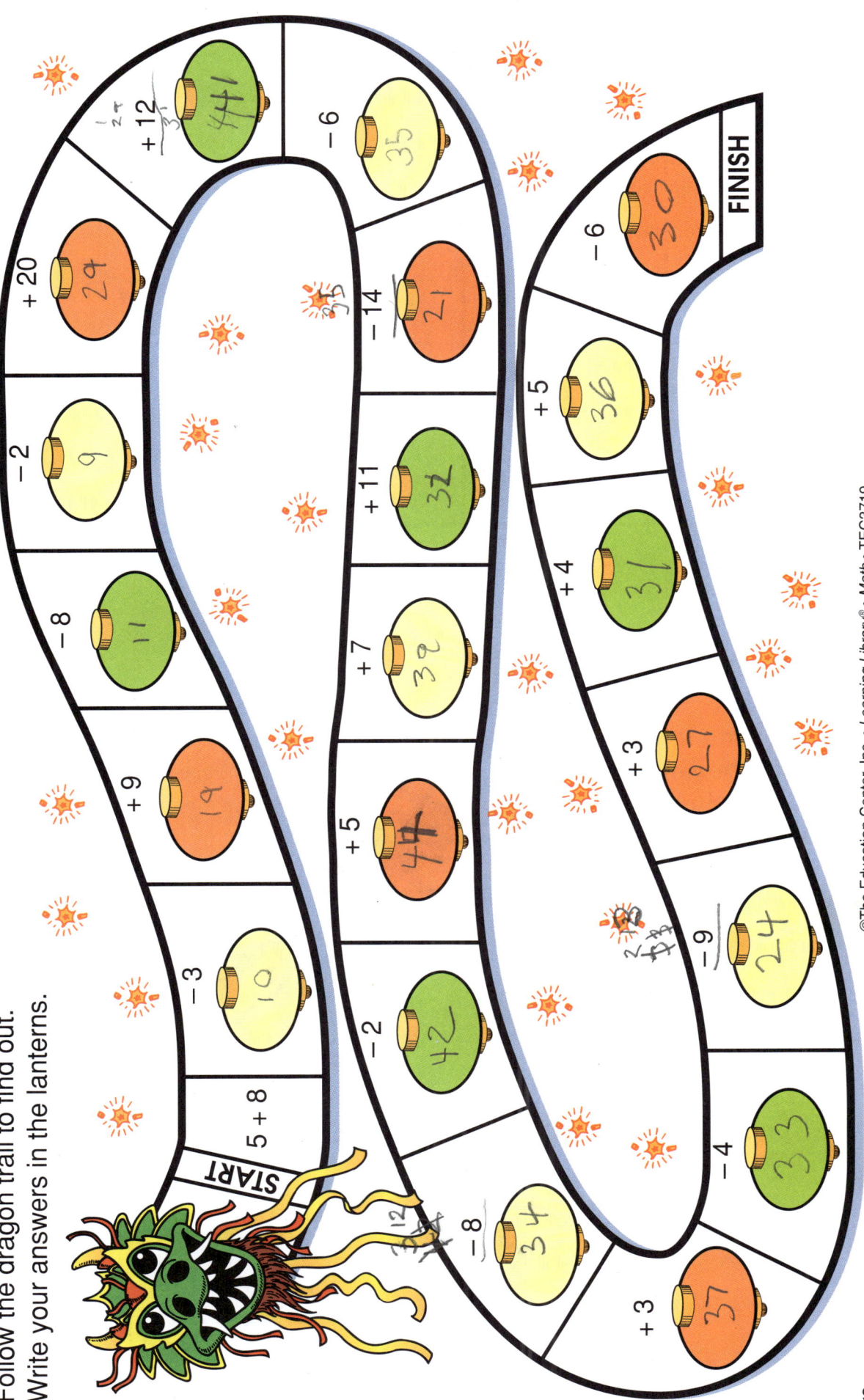

Bright Idea

Solve each problem.
See the example.

Example: 3 12 4̸2̸ − 19 ——— 23 = S	5 14 6̸4̸ − 38 ——— 26 = L	6 17 7̸7̸ − 29 ——— 48 = A	6 15 7̸5̸ − 46 ——— 29 = R	1 14 2̸4̸ − 17 ——— 07 = N
7 12 8̸2̸ − 33 ——— 49 = D	2 12 3̸2̸ − 16 ——— 16 = K	4 16 5̸6̸ − 9 ——— 47 = P	3 11 4̸1̸ − 17 ——— 24 = W	5 11 6̸1̸ − 24 ——— 37 = G
8 14 9̸4̸ − 86 ——— 08 = O	7 17 8̸7̸ − 8 ——— 79 = H	8 13 9̸3̸ − 39 ——— 54 = I	2 17 3̸7̸ − 9 ——— 28 = E	6 11 7̸1̸ − 33 ——— 38 = T

Use the code to solve the riddle.
What did the alligator invent to decorate his bathroom wall?

G L O W - I N - T H E - D A R K
37 26 8 24   54 7   38 79 28   49 48 29 16

" R E R - T I L E S "
  29 28 47   38 54 26 28 23

Name _____   Two-digit addition and subtraction with and without regrouping

A Trunk Full of Fun

Solve the problems.

95 − 73 = N	59 + 40 = S	81 − 57 = U	96 + 2 = M	98 − 43 = O
67 − 32 = M	79 + 11 = U	31 + 19 = R	89 − 62 = N	39 + 53 = W
71 − 28 = M	65 + 10 = R	55 − 26 = G	58 + 8 = S	49 + 45 = I	79 − 56 = T
65 + 22 = I	68 − 49 = S	32 + 12 = N	26 + 44 = O	58 − 25 = K	38 + 41 = E

To solve the riddle, match the letters to the numbered lines below.

What do you get when you cross an elephant with a fish?

__ __ __ __ __ __ __ __   __ __ __ __ __ __ __ __
79 22 70 50 35 55 24 19   99 92 94 43 98 87 27 29

                          __ __ __ __ __ __ !
                          23 75 90 44 33 66

In the Cornfield

Read each problem. Can you spot the clue words?
Write the answer in the blank.
Cross out each answer on the basket as you use it.
Look for **in all** or **all together**.
Then add.

1. Carl Crow ate 11 ears of corn.
   Crabby Crow ate 7 ears of corn.
   How many more ears did Carl eat? __4__

2. There are 8 crows in the cornfield.
   Four more crows will join them.
   How many crows will there be in all? __12__

3. One stalk of corn has 6 ears.
   Another stalk has 5 ears and another one has 3 ears.
   How many ears are there in all? __14__

4. There are 4 pumpkins in a row.
   There are 4 rows.
   How many pumpkins are there all together? __16__

5. Farmer Fred picked a lot of apples this week.
   He picked 7 baskets on Thursday and 5 baskets on Friday.
   He picked 8 baskets on Saturday.
   How many baskets did he pick in all? __20__

6. The scarecrow chased away 13 crows in the morning.
   He chased away 6 crows in the afternoon.
   How many crows were chased all together? __19__

7. The crows will eat 4 ears of corn for breakfast.
   They will eat 6 ears for lunch and 7 ears for dinner.
   How many ears will they eat in all? __17__

8. There are 5 stalks of corn in each row.
   There are 3 rows.
   How many stalks are there all together? __15__

9. The scarecrow has 13 buttons on his shirt.
   He has 4 buttons on his pants.
   How many more buttons are on his shirt? __9__

10. Farmer Fred will plant 16 rows of corn.
    He will plant 9 rows of pumpkins.
    How many more rows of corn will he have? __7__

Name _____

Word problems

Kick Up Your Heels!

**Read each problem carefully.
Underline the word or words that help you decide to add or subtract.
Solve the problem in the boot.**

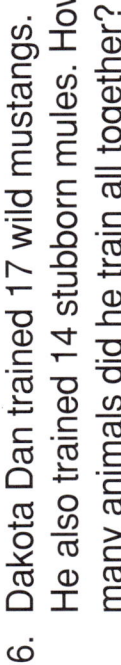
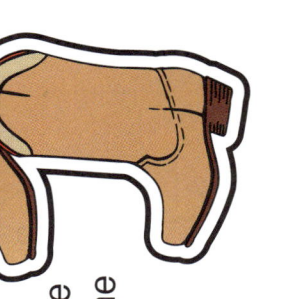

1. Cowboy Carl rounded up 46 cows. Tough Tex rounded up 27 more. How many cows were rounded up in all?

2. Chuck-Wagon Charlie made 78 biscuits. He served 29 of them. How many biscuits were left?

3. Lasso Lilly bought 34 horses for her ranch. She already had 36 horses. How many horses did she have all together?

4. Bronco Bill sold 83 rodeo tickets. Brother Bud sold 65 tickets. How many more tickets did Bronco Bill sell?

5. Tumbleweed Tess had 42 bales of hay. She used 26 bales to feed her cattle. How many bales did she have left?

6. Dakota Dan trained 17 wild mustangs. He also trained 14 stubborn mules. How many animals did he train all together?

7. Bowlegged Bob roped 32 ponies. Sagebrush Sue roped 27 ponies. How many more ponies did Bowlegged Bob rope?

8. Slim saw 51 coyotes howling at the moon. Then 45 of them fell asleep. How many coyotes were left howling?

9. Dusty counted 35 jackrabbits on the prairie. Rusty counted 16 more jackrabbits. How many jackrabbits were there in all?

10. Thunder Hoof threw 19 riders. Later he threw 23 more. How many riders did he throw in all?

Name_____ Subtraction: 3-digit with 1 regrouping

A Colorful Companion

Solve the problems. Show your work.
Color by the code.

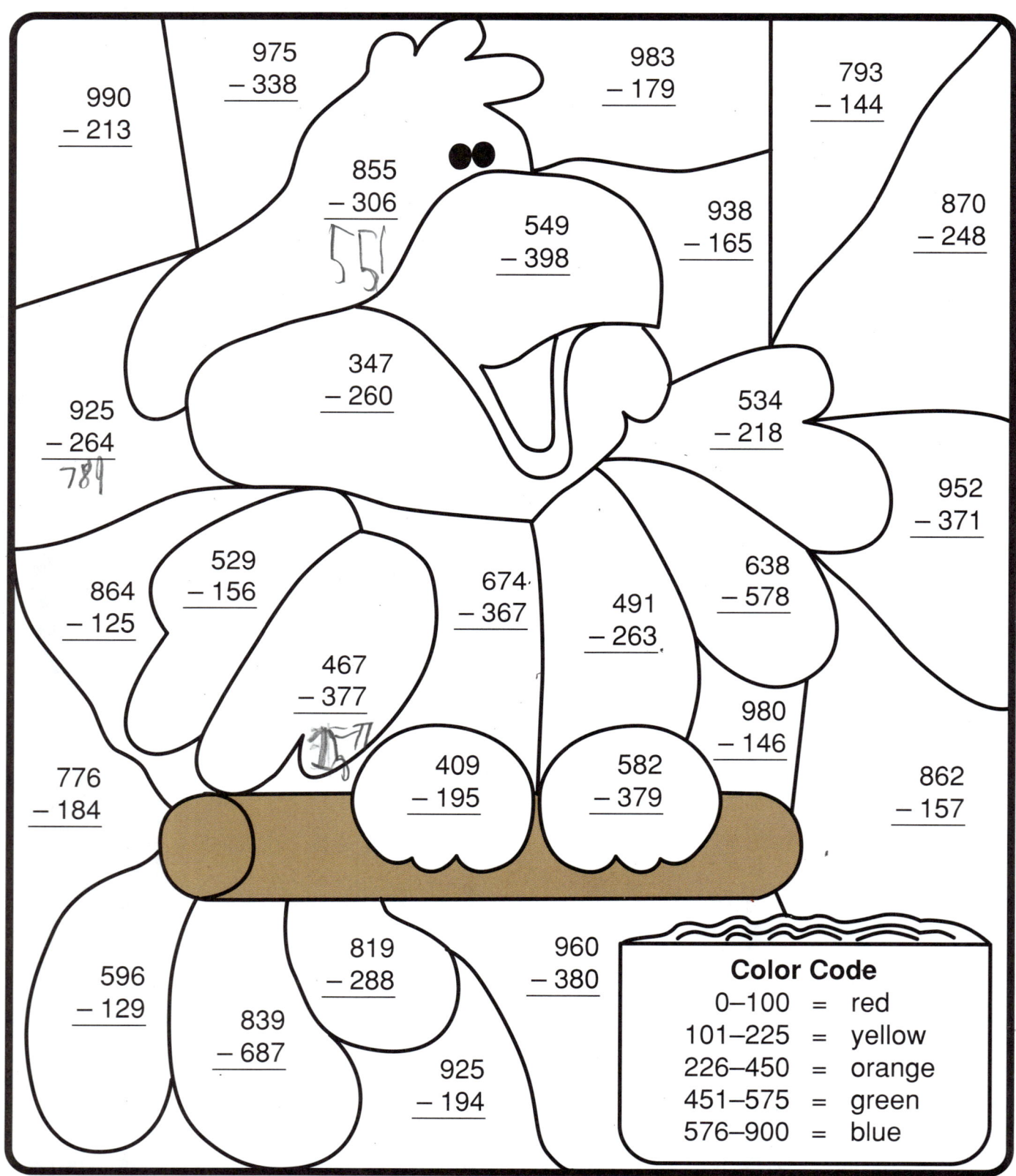

Color Code
0–100 = red
101–225 = yellow
226–450 = orange
451–575 = green
576–900 = blue

Name_____   Subtraction: 3-digit with 2 regroupings

A Playful Puppy

Solve the problems.
Show your work.

What should you do if your new puppy chews on a dictionary?

678 − 489 = K	496 − 197 = W	824 − 338 = O	427 − 249 = M	954 − 777 = F
286 − 189 = I	856 − 658 = T	531 − 278 = G	663 − 366 = E	721 − 382 = D
352 − 295 = H	725 − 576 = U	534 − 139 = A	521 − 364 = S	743 − 155 = R

To solve the riddle, match the letters to the numbered lines below.

__ __ __ __   __ __ __   __ __ __ __ __
198 395 189 297   198 57 297   299 486 588 339 157

__ __ __ __ __   __ __ __
588 97 253 57 198   486 149 198

__ __ __ __ __   __ __ __ __ __ !
486 177 97 198 157   178 486 149 198 57

©The Education Center, Inc. • Learning Library® • Math • TEC3719

Name_____   Subtraction: 3-digit with 2 regroupings

Fishy Friends

Solve each problem. Show your work.
If the answer on the fish is correct, color the fish.
If the answer is incorrect, copy and answer the problem on a blank fish.
Color, cut out, and glue that fish on top of the incorrect one.

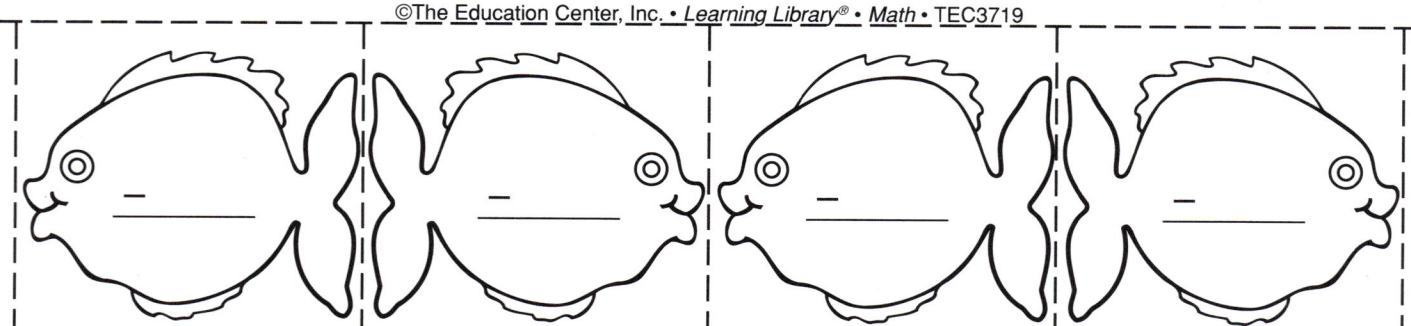

Name _____ Subtraction: 3-digit with 2 regroupings

Huggable Hamsters

Solve the problems. Show your work.
Color the answers in the maze.

Name_____   Subtraction: 3-digit with regrouping

A Salute to Subtraction

Solve each problem.
Circle each flag that shows a correct answer.

1. 743 − 307 — flags: 444, 436	2. 317 − 189 — flags: 128, 228	3. 436 − 238 — flags: 198, 202
4. 653 − 472 — flags: 185, 181	5. 727 − 586 — flags: 261, 141	6. 915 − 345 — flags: 570, 750
7. 274 − 156 — flags: 118, 128	8. 538 − 247 — flags: 371, 291	9. 624 − 586 — flags: 42, 38
10. 952 − 270 — flags: 722, 682	11. 467 − 174 — flags: 293, 393	12. 836 − 627 — flags: 209, 211

©The Education Center, Inc. • Learning Library® • Math • TEC3719

Name _____   Place value: Expanded notation

Popcorn Place Value

Write each number from 0 to 9 on a slip of paper.
Place them in a small brown bag.
For each set of questions, take three numbers from the bag.
Complete the work in each box.

Write the numerals on the popcorn.

1. What is the **largest** number that you can make with these numerals? _____

2. Write it in expanded notation. _____ + _____ + _____

3. What is the **smallest** number that you can make? _____

4. Write it in expanded notation. _____ + _____ + _____

Write the numerals on the popcorn.

5. What is the **largest** number that you can make with these numerals? _____

6. Write it in expanded notation. _____ + _____ + _____

7. What is the **smallest** number that you can make? _____

8. Write it in expanded notation. _____ + _____ + _____

Write the numerals on the popcorn.

9. What is the **largest** number that you can make with these numerals? _____

10. Write it in expanded notation. _____ + _____ + _____

11. What is the **smallest** number that you can make? _____

12. Write it in expanded notation. _____ + _____ + _____

Name_____   Counting by twos, threes, fives, and tens

Three Cheers for Numbers!

Help each cheerleader complete his or her cheer.
Fill in the missing numbers.

- 0, 2, ___, 6, ___, ___, 12, ___
- 52, ___, 56, 58, ___, ___, 64
- ___, 78, ___, 82, ___, 86, ___

- 5, ___, 15, ___, ___, 30, 35
- 45, ___, ___, 60, ___, ___, 75
- ___, 30, ___, ___, 45, 50, ___

- 6, ___, 12, ___, ___, 21, 24
- 33, ___, ___, 42, ___, 48, ___
- ___, 79, ___, ___, 88, 91, ___

- 0, ___, 20, 30, ___, ___, 60
- ___, 40, ___, 60, ___, 80, ___
- 20, ___, ___, 50, ___, ___, 80

Try This: Look at each cheerleader's cheer. Decide what number the cheerleader is counting by. Write the number on the cheerleader's sweater.

Name _____ Ordering numbers less than 100

Go, Team, Go!

Rewrite each set of numbers.
Order the numbers from the least to the greatest.

Megaphone 1:
55 ____
62 ____
14 ____
46 ____
87 ____

Megaphone 2:
4 ____
43 ____
64 ____
46 ____
34 ____

Megaphone 3:
92 ____
7 ____
89 ____
4 ____
96 ____

Megaphone 4:
42 ____
65 ____
53 ____
71 ____
34 ____

Megaphone 5:
16 ____
8 ____
32 ____
54 ____
48 ____

Megaphone 6:
20 ____
6 ____
26 ____
66 ____
62 ____

Megaphone 7:
35 ____
42 ____
68 ____
27 ____
124 ____

Megaphone 8:
82 ____
86 ____
81 ____
87 ____
84 ____

Megaphone 9:
18 ____
25 ____
15 ____
8 ____
35 ____

Try This: Circle the odd numbers in red. Draw a blue box around the even numbers.

Name _____   Number order: Sequencing numbers less than 1,000

Spider Sprints

These spiders are getting ready to have a race. Help them line up.
For each row, write the numerals in order from the lowest to the highest.

A. 651 156 615 516

___ ___ ___ ___

B. 437 213 440 537

___ ___ ___ ___

C. 616 166 669 606

___ ___ ___ ___

D. 111 201 109 209

309 409 ~~509~~ 609

E. 80 28 82 280

___ ___ ___ ___

F. 888 953 980 818

___ ___ ___ ___

Name_____ Place value: Ones, tens, hundreds

A Place to Stay

Name the place value of each underlined digit.
Write the room key number on the matching building.

Room Key Numbers

74*2*
2*1*9
3*8*
*1*06
78*1*
2*4*
45*5*
*6*97
36*3*
5*6*0
*5*54
*3*07
8*3*5
*7*2
92*6*
*2*41
47*9*
1*1*0
*8*08
63*3*
*9*24
*5*90
78*8*
*2*17
*9*95
*8*62
*5*1
*3*43
17*6*
*4*89
5*8*
93*3*
*1*24
*7*5

Name _____ Place value: Ones, tens, hundreds

All Aboard!

Use the numerals boarding each bus to make six three-digit numbers.
Write the numbers on the lines.

Draw a purple circle around the largest number on each bus.
Draw a green box around the smallest number on each bus.

At Home: Roll a die three times. Write each number. Combine the numerals to make six numbers. Who can write the biggest number?

Name_____ Place value: Ones through thousands

Picture-Perfect Places

Use the information in each picture frame to make a number.
Write each number on the matching line below.

A.	B.	C.	D.
9 ones	1 hundred	7 tens	5 thousands
2 thousands	4 thousands	2 ones	2 hundreds
3 tens	0 tens	9 hundreds	5 ones
5 hundreds	6 ones	1 thousand	8 tens

E.	F.	G.	H.
5 tens	7 hundreds	7 thousands	0 ones
4 hundreds	2 tens	8 hundreds	6 hundreds
9 thousands	3 thousands	6 tens	4 tens
8 ones	1 one	3 ones	8 thousands

I.	J.	K.	L.
3 hundreds	9 tens	5 ones	1 thousand
1 ten	7 ones	0 tens	3 ones
4 ones	3 thousands	0 hundreds	7 tens
6 thousands	1 hundred	5 thousands	2 hundreds

M.	N.
3 tens	9 hundreds
9 thousands	4 thousands
2 ones	8 ones
6 hundreds	5 tens

Number Box

A. _____   H. Hundreds

B. _____   I. _____

C. _____   J. _____

D. _____   K. _____

E. _____   L. _____

F. _____   M. _____

G. _____   N. _____

2,539

Welcome to **Digit Falls**

Try This: Put a comma between the hundreds and thousands.

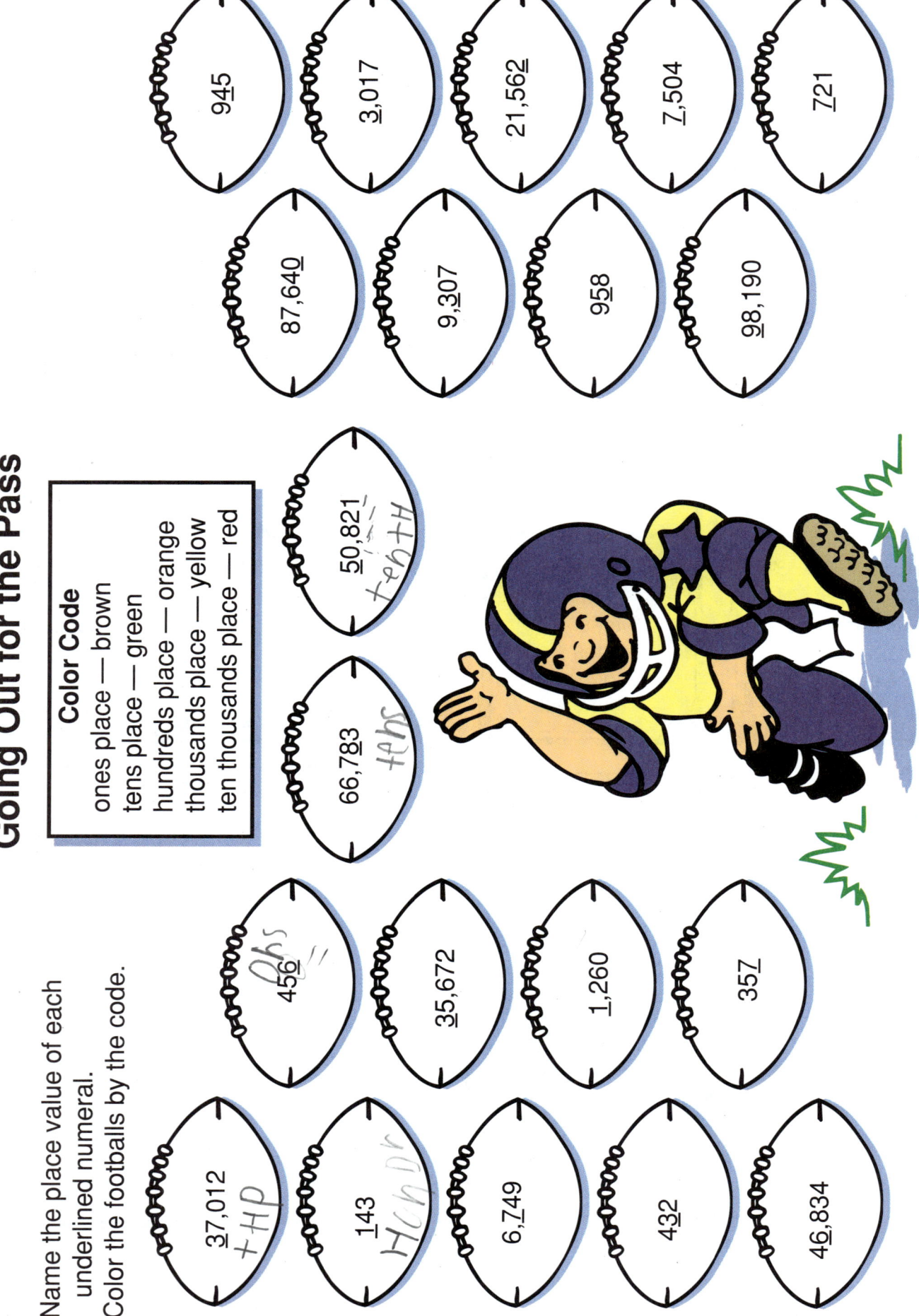

Name _____   Addition: 3-digit without regrouping

Pet Palace

Solve each problem.
Cross out the matching answer in the Answer Bank.

a. 433
   + 462

b. 157
   + 721

c. 423
   + 325

d. 830
   + 159

Answer Bank

559
578
695
748
769
794
869
878
895
899
958
967
968
986
989
996

e. 126
   + 832

f. 574
   + 121

g. 263
   + 506

h. 415
   + 553

i. 613
   + 383

j. 324
   + 470

k. 257
   + 642

l. 542
   + 444

m. 736
   + 231

n. 128
   + 450

o. 646
   + 223

p. 355
   + 204

Two-for-One Sale!

Name_____ Addition: 3-digit with regrouping

Getting to the Heart of the Problem

Follow the steps.
Solve the problems.

To add 3-digit numbers you may need to *regroup* the tens and hundreds.

- First, add the ones. If the answer is more than 10, *regroup the ones.*
  For example, the 12 ones are regrouped to make another group of 10 and a group of 2.
- Next, write 1 above the tens place.
- Write the 2 in the ones place.
- Add all the tens.
- Then add the hundreds.

Example:

```
  1
 646      522      789      561      357
+206     +460     +276     +441     +622
 852


 434      959      643      849      603
+553     +113     +141     +227     +272


 689      424      121      790      874
+132     +322     +854     +350     +653


 719      959      184      573      853
+160     +453     +714     +303     +532
```

If the answer is **even**, draw a red heart around it.

```
 367      316
+234     +453
```

If the answer is **odd**, draw a purple heart around it.

At Home: Save those cash register receipts! Circle two items between $1.99 and $9.00 on the receipt. Write an addition problem. (Demonstrate how to line up the decimal points to add.) Use pennies to model the ones and dimes for the tens. Regroup pennies to make tens. Trade ten pennies for a dime. Repeat the practice.

Name _____   Addition with regrouping

Migrating Problems

Gordon Goose is traveling south for the winter.
Find how many miles Gordon will travel.
Solve each problem using the map below.
Show your work.

How many miles is it from

1. Mount Freeze to Rainytown? +_____	2. Coldville to Misty Valley? +_____	3. Rainytown to Middleburg? +_____
4. Middleburg to Sunshine Land? +_____	5. Pleasant City to Hot Town? +_____	6. Sunshine Land to Summer Beach? +_____

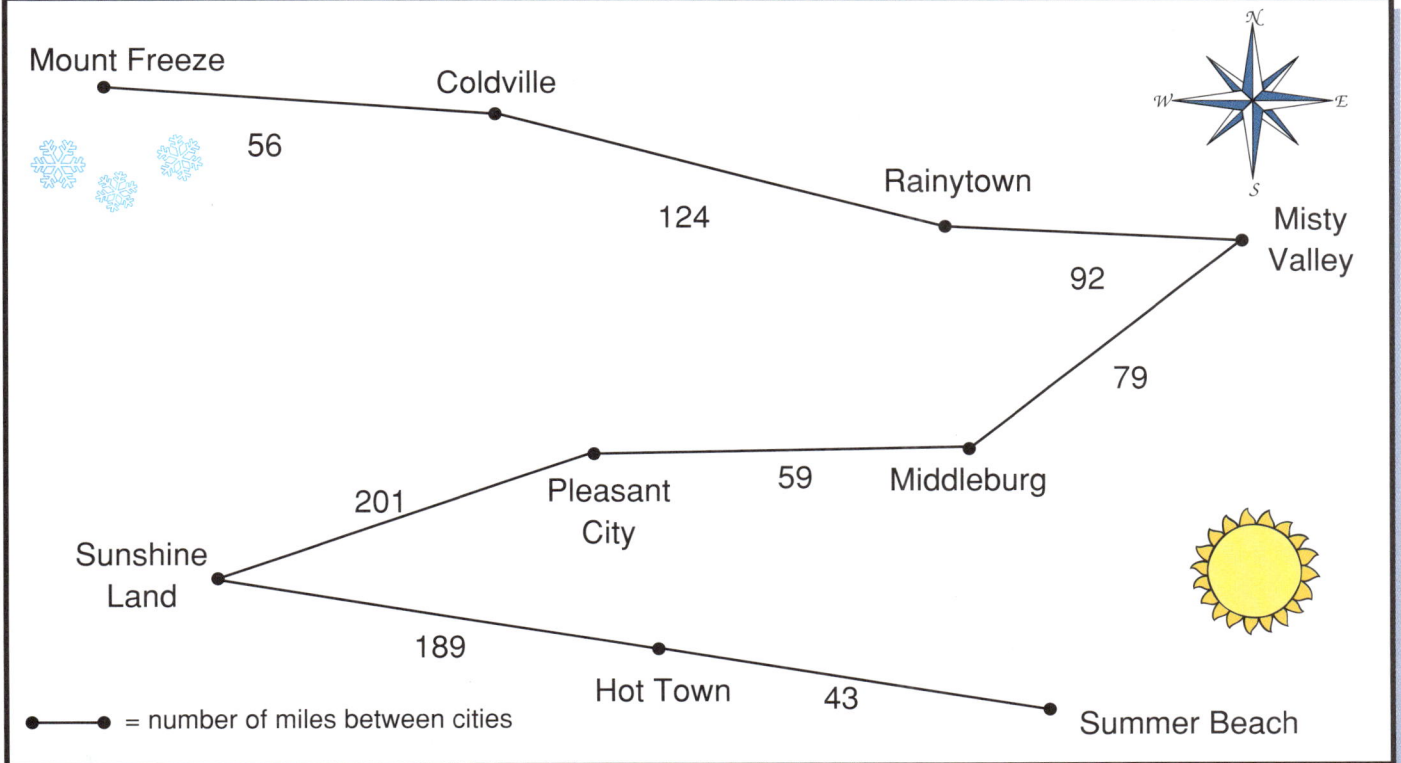

•—• = number of miles between cities

At Home: Provide a road map. Help your child find the distance between two towns.

Name _____ Addition: 3-digit with regrouping

The Music Box

Solve each problem. Show your work.
If the answer on the note is correct, color the note.

a. 554 + 153 = 707
b. 438 + 523 = 951
c. 637 + 238 = 885
d. 264 + 194 = 458
e. 362 + 545 = 807

f. 172 + 595 = 777
g. 416 + 215 = 631
h. 578 + 231 = 809
i. 319 + 345 = 654

j. 376 + 452 = 728
k. 681 + 157 = 837
l. 493 + 195 = 688
m. 459 + 460 = 819
n. 348 + 638 = 986

o. 495 + 233 = 728
p. 827 + 147 = 975
q. 385 + 194 = 589
r. 267 + 272 = 539

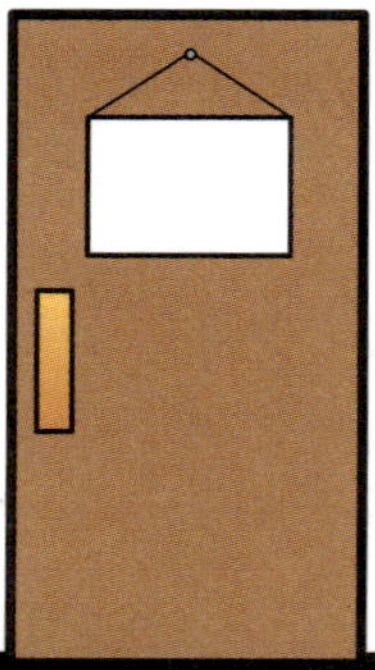

Name _____   Subtraction: 3-digit without regrouping

The Candy Jar

Solve the problems.

a. 697 − 610

b. 587 − 432

c. 897 − 567

d. 764 − 453

e. 743 − 500

f. 488 − 214

g. 365 − 122

h. 425 − 121

i. 476 − 225

j. 697 − 423

k. 989 − 685

l. 956 − 753

m. 592 − 341

n. 788 − 701

o. 939 − 533

p. 467 − 264

q. 869 − 463

r. 958 − 803

s. 659 − 329

t. 543 − 232

For each gumdrop, find another gumdrop with the same answer.
Color the matching gumdrops exactly the same.
Use as many colors as you like.

Name _____   Subtraction: 3-digit with regrouping

Math-ola Crayons

Look at the example.
Solve the problems.
Color by the code.

- yellow: less than 100
- blue: 100–200
- purple: 200–400
- green: 400–600
- red: more than 600

Example:
$$\begin{array}{r}\overset{2\ 14\ 12}{\cancel{352}} \\ -184 \\ \hline 168 \end{array}$$

A. 642 − 178
B. 770 − 382
C. 923 − 504
D. 831 − 158
E. 910 − 777
F. 790 − 146
G. 596 − 247
H. 672 − 347
I. 975 − 877

Follow the steps.

To subtract **3-digit numbers:**
- First subtract in the ones place.
  Regroup the tens to get more ones like this:
  Subtract the ones.

- Regroup the hundreds to get more tens like this:
  Then, subtract in the tens place.

- Subtract the hundreds.
  The difference between 352 and 184 is 168.

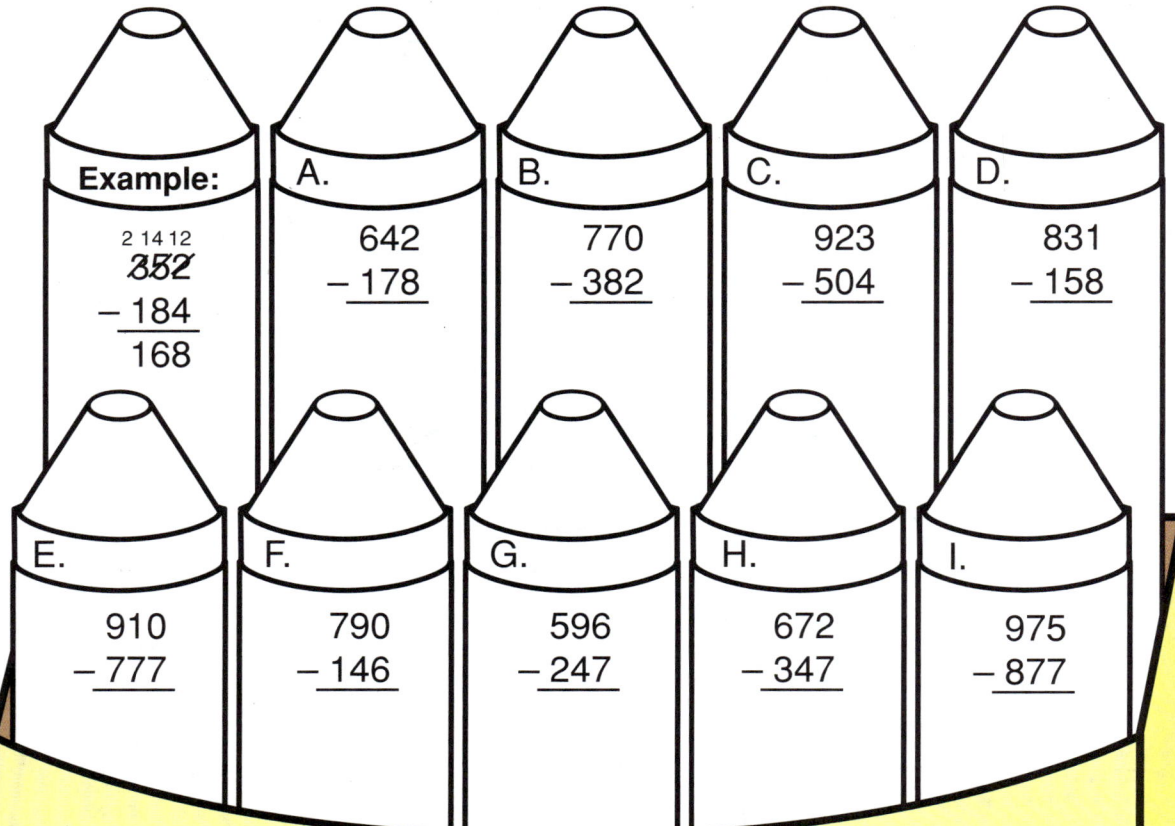

Name_____

Subtraction: 3-digit with regrouping across zeros

Subtraction Brushup

Look at the example. Follow the steps. Solve the problems. Color by the code on page 32.

A. 600 − 273

B. 500 − 38

C. 800 − 256

D. 300 − 48

E. 400 − 163

F. 700 − 640

G. 900 − 256

H. 900 − 809

I. 300 − 123

J. 900 − 256

K. 800 − 608

To subtract from **3-digit numbers with zeros:**

To get more tens, you must regroup the hundreds like this:

Then regroup (or borrow from) the tens to get more ones like this:

- Now you can subtract the ones.
- Next, if you need more tens, regroup the hundreds.
- Subtract from the tens.
- Then subtract from what's left of the hundreds.
- The difference between 500 and 295 is 205.

$$\begin{array}{r} \overset{4}{\cancel{5}}\overset{9}{\cancel{0}}\overset{10}{\cancel{0}} \\ -\ 295 \\ \hline 205 \end{array}$$

At Home: Working with money is a great way to practice subtraction across zeros. Look in the newspaper to find an item that costs under $5.00. Have your child subtract to find how much money he would have left if you gave him a five-dollar bill to purchase the item.

Name _____   Subtraction: 3-digit with regrouping

The Computer Connection

Solve each problem. Show your work.
Cross out the matching answer in the keyboard.

Example:

a. $\overset{2\ 14}{5\cancel{3}\cancel{4}}$
   -218
   _____

b. 952
   -371
   _____

c. 467
   -377
   _____

d. 582
   -379
   _____

e. 925
   -264
   _____

f. 409
   -195
   _____

g. 596
   -129
   _____

h. 864
   -125
   _____

i. 690
   -313
   _____

j. 793
   -144
   _____

k. 376
   -284
   _____

l. 760
   -580
   _____

m. 749
   -498
   _____

n. 875
   -238
   _____

o. 855
   -306
   _____

p. 927
   -192
   _____

q. 483
   -259
   _____

r. 862
   -457
   _____

s. 729
   -256
   _____

t. 839
   -687
   _____

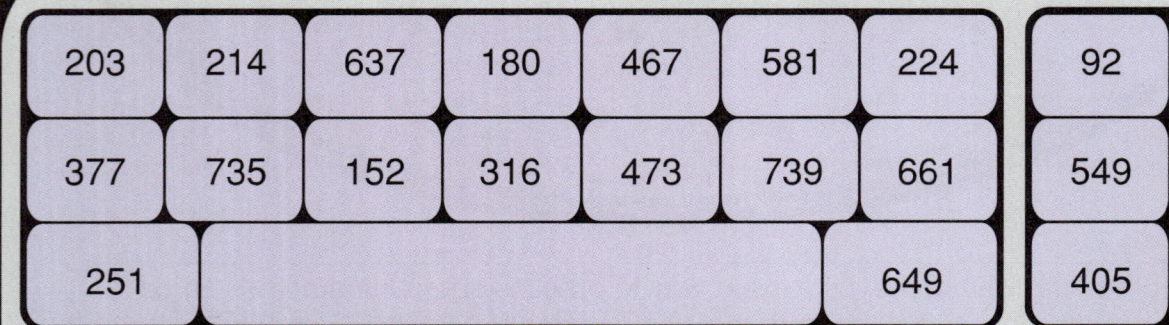

Name _____ Addition/subtraction: Mixed practice

Mouse Match

Solve each problem.
For each computer mouse, find the real mouse with the same answer.
Color the matching mice the same color.
Use a different color for each pair of mice.

1. 534
   −219

2. 319
   +345

3. 876
   −285

4. 172
   +687

5. 896
   −232

6. 193
   +447

7. 544
   +307

8. 119
   +196

9. 409
   −195

10. 270
   +321

11. 991
   −132

12. 733
   − 93

13. 958
   −107

14. 217
   +498

15. 119
   + 95

16. 897
   −182

©The Education Center, Inc. • Learning Library® • Math • TEC3719

Name _____   Multiplication facts

Want to Add *Really* Fast? Multiply!

When you *multiply,* you are **adding equal groups** together or repeating groups of the same number.

For example: 3 groups of 2 equals 2 + 2 + 2.
You write 3 x 2 = 6 or   3
                        x 2

                          6

(You say, "Three times two equals six.")
The *X* means multiply.
The answer (6) is called the *product.*
3 and 2 are called *factors.*

Now find the product of 4 x 4. Think of 4 + 4 + 4 + 4.
Or think of four rows of four like this pattern, or *array:*

* * * *
* * * *
* * * *
* * * *

Multiplication is a really fast addition!

You can add over and over to get 16, or you can multiply! To multiply really fast, you need to memorize all the facts shown on the times table.

1. 4 x 3 = _____
2. 5 x 5 = _____
3. 6 x 6 = _____
4. 7 x 3 = _____
5. 8 x 7 = _____

x	0	1	2	3	4	5	6	7	8	9
0	0	0	0	0	0	0	0	0	0	0
1	0	1	2	3	4	5	6	7	8	9
2	0	2	4	6	8	10	12	14	16	18
3	0	3	6	9	12	15	18	21	24	27
4	0	4	8	12	16	20	24	28	32	36
5	0	5	10	15	20	25	30	35	40	45
6	0	6	12	18	24	30	36	42	48	54
7	0	7	14	21	28	35	42	49	56	63
8	0	8	16	24	32	40	48	56	64	72
9	0	9	18	27	36	45	54	63	72	81

At Home: To help you memorize all the facts, make your own flash cards from 3" x 5" cards. Label each card with two factors and their product. Start with the twos, threes, and fours. Don't forget to make cards for zero times each factor, zero through nine!

Name _____ Multiplication

A Bunch of Multiplication!

Farmer Fred has a bumper crop of carrots. He wants to sell them in bunches. Help Fred decide how many carrots to pick.

Here's an example:
How many carrots does Fred need to make 4 bunches of 8?

Choose a strategy:
You can draw an *array* to show 4 bunches of 8.

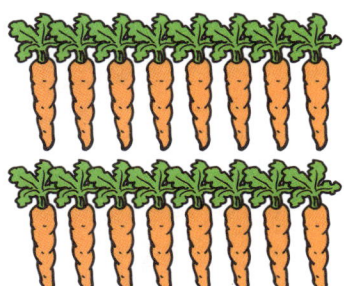 

Or you can add 8 + 8 + 8 + 8.
Or you can write 4 x 8 = 32 or   4
                                 x 8
                                ____
                                 32 carrots

Write the equation and multiply to find how many carrots Fred needs to make

1. 5 bunches of 6   5 x 6 = ____
2. 6 bunches of 5   6 x 5 = ____
3. 8 bunches of 4   _____
4. 8 bunches of 6   _____
5. 9 bunches of 4   _____
6. 4 bunches of 6   _____
7. 7 bunches of 5   _____
8. 8 bunches of 5   _____
9. 7 bunches of 8   _____
10. 1 jumbo bunch of 32 _____

Try This: Practice your multiplication facts by planning a sleepover! Choose a number of guests to invite from two to nine. (Check with your parents first.) How many doughnuts will you need if each person eats four? How much milk will you all drink if each person drinks two glasses? How many times will you all play a favorite game if everyone plays the game three times? How many pancakes will you need to cook if you each eat five? (Don't forget to count yourself!)

Name_____ Multiplication: Basic facts: 0–5

New Tire Needed

Fanny Flamingo needs your help!
Multiply each number on the tire by the center number.
One answer is done for you.

Size A — ×4, numbers: 5, 9, 6, 8, 4, 7, 1, 3 (1 × 4 = 4)

Size B — ×3, numbers: 3, 7, 0, 5, 6, 4, 8, 9

Size C — ×2, numbers: 2, 6, 7, 4, 9, 5, 8, 3

Size D — ×1, numbers: 3, 6, 9, 7, 2, 4, 5, 1

Size E — ×0, numbers: 0, 7, 9, 5, 8, 6, 4, 2

Find the tire that has the same answers as Fanny's flat.
Color this tire pink!

Size F — ×5, numbers: 6, 5, 7, 2, 3, 8, 9, 4

Flat tire numbers: 24, 16, 4, 36, 28, 20, 12, 32

Try This: Flamingo tires come in 6 sizes. They have 4 of each size in stock. How many tires in all?

Name_____ Multiplication: Basic facts: 6–7

Lift and Look

For each letter, write a problem that equals the answer on the pole. Each problem must be a factor of 6 or 7. Solve the problem.

a. ☐ x ☐   b. ☐ x ☐   c. ☐ x ☐   d. ☐ x ☐

a.	14
b.	18
c.	28
d.	54
e.	49
f.	36
g.	21
h.	0
i.	6
j.	42
k.	48
l.	56
m.	35
n.	12
o.	30
p.	63
q.	7
r.	24
s.	0
t.	42

e. ☐ x ☐   f. ☐ x ☐   g. ☐ x ☐   h. ☐ x ☐

i. ☐ x ☐   j. ☐ x ☐   k. ☐ x ☐   l. ☐ x ☐

m. ☐ x ☐   n. ☐ x ☐   o. ☐ x ☐   p. ☐ x ☐

q. ☐ x ☐   r. ☐ x ☐   s. ☐ x ☐   t. ☐ x ☐

Try This: Frank's Flamingo Auto Repair is open 6 days a week. How many days does Frank work in a month?

Name _____   Multiplication: Basic facts: 7–9

Ready to Repair

Use the code.
Write each missing factor.
Solve each problem.

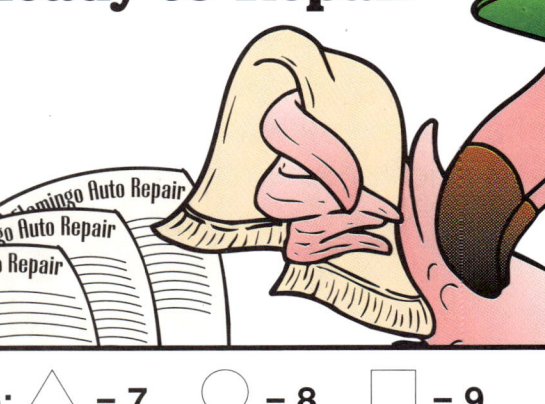

Code: △ = 7   ○ = 8   □ = 9

a. △ x 7 = ____   9 x □ = ____   □ x 4 = ____

b. 2   △   3   ○   6   □   ○
   x○   x 8   x□   x 9   x△   x 8   x 5

c. 2 x □ = ____   7 x ○ = ____   ○ x 4 = ____

d. △   5   □   ○   △   ○   5
   x 4   x△   x 7   x 1   x 2   x 8   x□

e. □ x 6 = ____   7 x △ = ____   9 x ○ = ____

f. 1   ○   5   3   □   5   △
   x△   x 6   x□   x△   x 1   x○   x 9

40   ©The Education Center, Inc. • Learning Library® • Math • TEC3719

Name _____   Multiplication: Basic facts: 10–12

Fill 'er Up!

It has been a very busy day at Flamingo Fuel & Auto Repair!
Find the total of each gas ticket.
Use the prices on the gas pump.

A. Best Gas — Three gallons	**B.** Cheap Gas — Five gallons
C. Cheap Gas — Eight gallons	**D.** Good Gas — Six gallons
E. Best Gas — Ten gallons	**F.** Cheap Gas — Four gallons
G. Good Gas — Nine gallons	**H.** Cheap Gas — Twelve gallons
I. Best Gas — Seven gallons	**J.** Good Gas — Eleven gallons
K. Good Gas — Two gallons	**L.** Best Gas — Five gallons

Gas Pump — Flamingo Fuel — $00.00

Best Gas = 12¢ per gallon
Good Gas = 11¢ per gallon
Cheap Gas = 10¢ per gallon

Bonus Box: Color each ticket.
Pink = total is more than 75¢
Yellow = total is less than 75¢

Name_____   Multiplication facts: Missing factors 0–5

Searching for Shadows

Use the numbers on the suns and clouds to complete the facts. Color each sun or cloud as you use its number. Are there more clouds than suns?

Row A

| 7 × □ = 7 | □ × 6 = 0 | □ × 1 = 3 | 2 × □ = 6 | □ × 3 = 15 | 8 × □ = 16 |

Row B

| □ × 4 = 12 | 8 × □ = 40 | 7 × □ = 14 | 9 × □ = 36 | □ × 4 = 20 | □ × 1 = 3 |

Row C

| 9 × □ = 27 | □ × 5 = 25 | 5 × □ = 10 | □ × 8 = 8 | 6 × □ = 12 | □ × 3 = 9 |

Row D

| □ × 7 = 35 | □ × 7 = 28 | 7 × □ = 21 | □ × 9 = 18 | 4 × □ = 8 | 9 × □ = 45 |

Row E

| □ × 4 = 16 | 3 × □ = 12 | | | 6 × □ = 24 | □ × 2 = 0 |

Will it be sunny or cloudy?

44   ©The Education Center, Inc. • Learning Library® • Math • TEC3719

Something to Howl About

Solve each problem.

8	6	2	9	3	4	5	7
x 5	x 8	x 2	x 8	x 7	x 1	x 3	x 8

8	4	6	2	7	9	3	7
x 2	x 4	x 4	x 3	x 2	x 4	x 6	x 1

5	6	3	7	4	6	7	4
x 5	x 0	x 8	x 7	x 0	x 6	x 9	x 2

6	8	5	4	6	4	3	5
x 2	x 4	x 7	x 7	x 5	x 9	x 4	x 8

Try This: How old are you in dog years?

Multiply your age by 7!

Name_____ Division: Parts of a set

Decorate With Division

Help Mr. Cookie divide his delicious decorations evenly by drawing a ring around each group. The first one is done for you.

12 chocolate chips divided between 3 cookies = 4 chips on each cookie
12 ÷ 3 = 4

1. 12 chips ÷ 4 cookies = _____
    12 ÷ 4 = _____

2. 6 cherries ÷ 6 cookies = _____
    6 ÷ 6 = _____

3. 10 raisins ÷ 5 rolls = _____
    10 ÷ 5 = _____

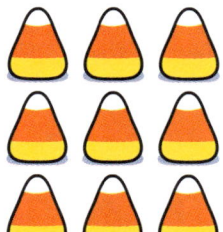

4. 14 ÷ 2 = _____

5. 9 ÷ 3 = _____

6. 8 ÷ 4 = _____

7. 3 ÷ 1 = _____

8. 4 ÷ 2 = _____

10. 15 ÷ 3 = _____

9. 16 ÷ 4 = _____

At Home: Try dealing different numbers of playing cards evenly among different numbers of players.

46   ©The Education Center, Inc. • Learning Library® • Math • TEC3719

Name_____   Division: Word problems

How Does Your Garden Grow?

You are planting a garden.
Show your work as you solve the problems.

1. You have 49 tomato plants. You want to divide them evenly among 7 rows in your garden. How many tomato plants should be in each row?

2. 27 squash seeds come in a package. If you plant 3 seeds in each hole, how many holes are there?

3. Last year your garden yielded 48 potatoes. If there were 8 plants with the same number of potatoes, how many potatoes grew on each plant?

4. If you want to increase your yield to 60 potatoes this year, how many plants will you need?

5. You usually divide your carrots into bunches of 6. If you harvest 36 carrots, how many bunches will you have?

6. You have 30 watermelon seeds. If you plant 10 in each row, how many rows will you have?

7. When weeding your garden, you found 6 beetles. There was the same number of beetles on each of 6 dandelions. How many beetles were on each dandelion?

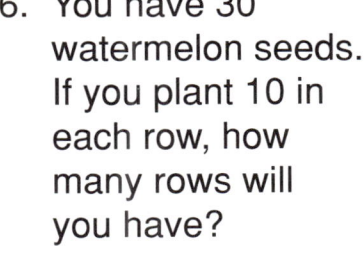

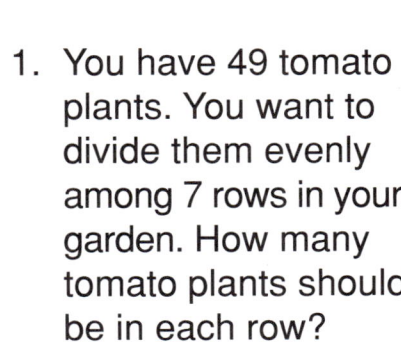

Third-Grade Parent Page

Fractions and Measurements

Your child already has an understanding of fractions from first and second grade. She understands equal parts of a whole unit. In third grade, she will see fractions as parts of whole units, parts of collections, and as locations on a number line. *Numerator* and *denominator* become part of her math vocabulary. There will be plenty of practice with recipes and sharing in the classroom. She will use *equivalent forms*, such as 2/4 = 1/2, to judge the size of fractions. This can be tricky at first, as your child wonders how 1/3 can be more than 1/6 if 6 is more than 3!

Your third grader understands the need to measure in standard units and to compare measurements in the same units. She'll use both customary and *metric* units to measure length, width, and capacity. She'll be able to make simple conversions, such as feet to yards and centimeters to meters. As she begins to measure and compare length, width, area, volume, capacity, and temperature, she'll begin to estimate reasonable measurements and decide when precise measurements are not needed.

Third graders should be able to
- measure length in inches, feet, meters, and centimeters
- find perimeter in inches and centimeters
- understand the concept of area
- measure capacity using cups, pints, quarts, and gallons
- estimate weight in pounds, ounces, and metric units of weight
- compare degrees Fahrenheit and Celsius
- identify the appropriate tool needed to find weight, volume, length, width, height, and temperature
- identify fractional parts of a whole and of a collection
- solve word problems with fractions

Key Math Skills for Grade 3
Fractions and Measurements

- Fractions: recognizing and comparing parts of a whole
- Fractions: identifying fractional parts
- Fractions: identifying parts of a group (2/5 of 15 balls)
- Fractions: solving word problems with fractions
- Measurement: choosing the appropriate measuring tool
- Measurement: measuring length in inches or centimeters
- Measurement: finding perimeter in inches and centimeters
- Measurement: finding area in centimeters
- Temperature: comparing degrees Celsius and Fahrenheit
- Weight: estimating pounds and ounces
- Weight: estimating metric units
- Capacity: estimating capacity in cups, pints, quarts, and gallons

Shop Till You Drop

Include your child in the everyday challenge of shopping. Explore the shelf stickers for ounces and price per ounce. Weigh the produce. Compare package or container sizes to find the best values. You'll gain by teaching your child to be a smart shopper.

Sick Day

Feeling better? A common cold is a great opportunity for reinforcing measurement skills. Take your child's temperature and have her record it in degrees. Ask, "Do you have a fever? How close is this to 98.6°F?" Then explore eyedroppers, medicine cups, and measuring spoons and compare these small units of capacity. Ask, "Why is it important to measure the correct dosage of medicine?"

Name _____ Fractions: Parts of a whole

A Slice of Everything!

Pizza? Brownies? Watermelon? Cake?
Peppy Panda loves to have "just a slice" (or two) of *everything* on the pizza parlor menu! Write the fraction for each shaded section.

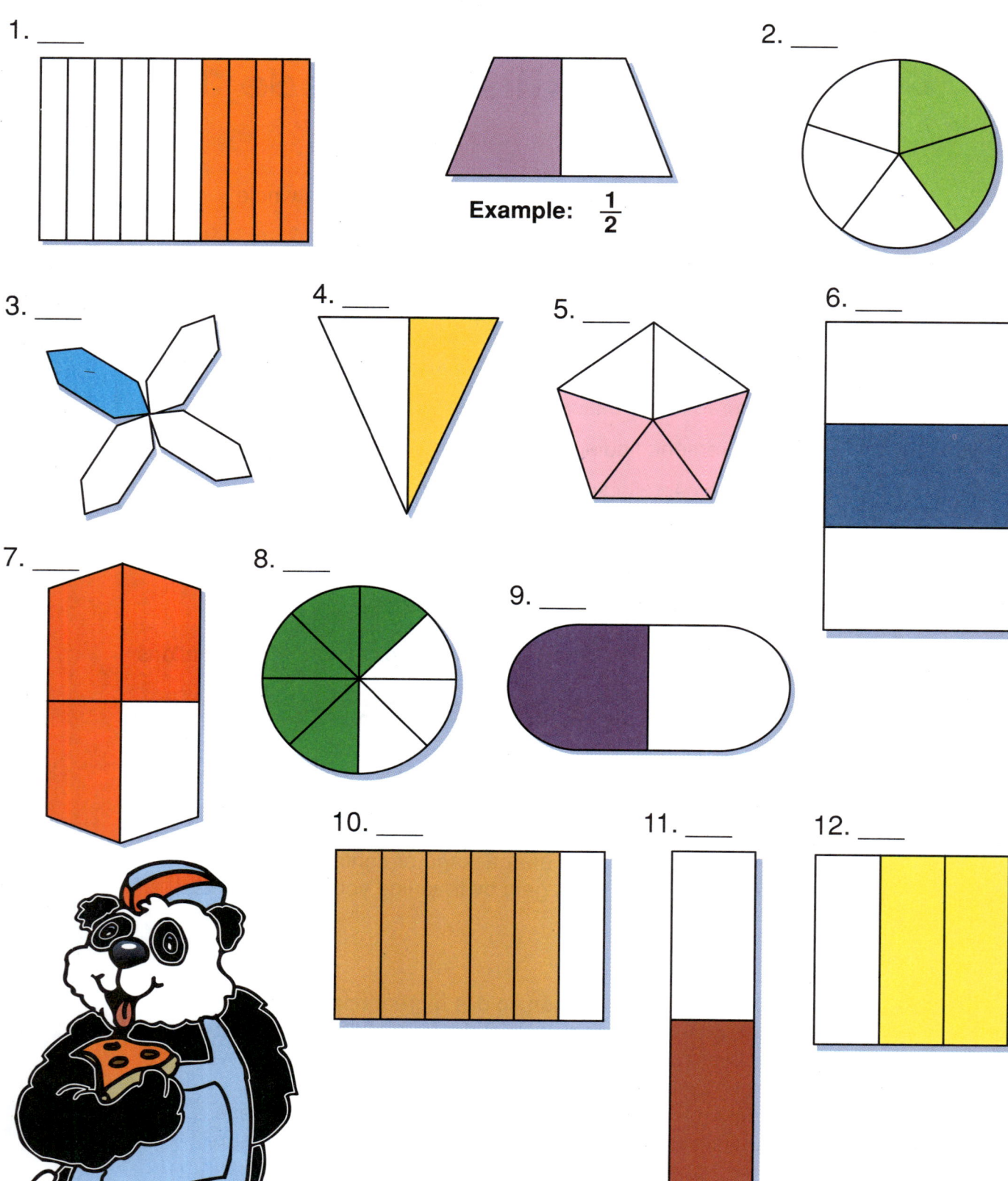

50 ©The Education Center, Inc. • Learning Library® • Math • TEC3719

Name _____ Fractions: Increasing a recipe

Panda's Pizzeria

Panda's pantry has plenty of ingredients for pizza.
He wants to **double** the recipe.
How much will he need for two pizzas?

Panda's Pepperoni Pizza

2 c. flour   ½ tsp. salt   1 c. tomato sauce
¾ c. warm water   ½ tsp. sugar   oregano
2 tsp. dry yeast   2 Tbsp. oil   ½ c. grated mozzarella cheese
                                       ¼ pepperoni stick

Dissolve yeast in warm water. Stir in sugar, salt, oil, and 1¾ cup flour. Mix to make a soft dough, adding flour as needed. Flatten dough on a pizza pan. Spread with 1 cup tomato sauce. Sprinkle with oregano. Top with ½ cup grated mozzarella cheese and ¼ pepperoni stick sliced thin. Bake at 425° for 20 minutes. (Makes 1 pizza.)

Color the measuring cups to show how much flour and cheese for two pizzas. Write how much.

How much for two?

____ tsp. dry yeast

____ tsp. salt

____ Tbsp. oil

____ cups of flour   ____ cups of mozzarella cheese

Draw how many cups of water below. Write how much.

____ cups of water

Color the pepperoni needed for two pizzas.

At Home: Make a batch of pizza dough according to the recipe. Double it for two pizzas!

Name _____   Fractions: Identifying fractional parts

Lots of Leftovers

Cut out each pizza.
Decide how much of the pizza is left.
Glue the pizza on its matching pan.

1/3	○	1/4	○	2/3	○
3/8	○	1/5	○	2/6	○
1/2	○	4/6	○	1/8	○
3/4	○	2/5	○	4/4	○

Try This: Peppy Panda had the least amount of pizza left on her pizza pan. Use a yellow crayon to circle Peppy's pizza pan.

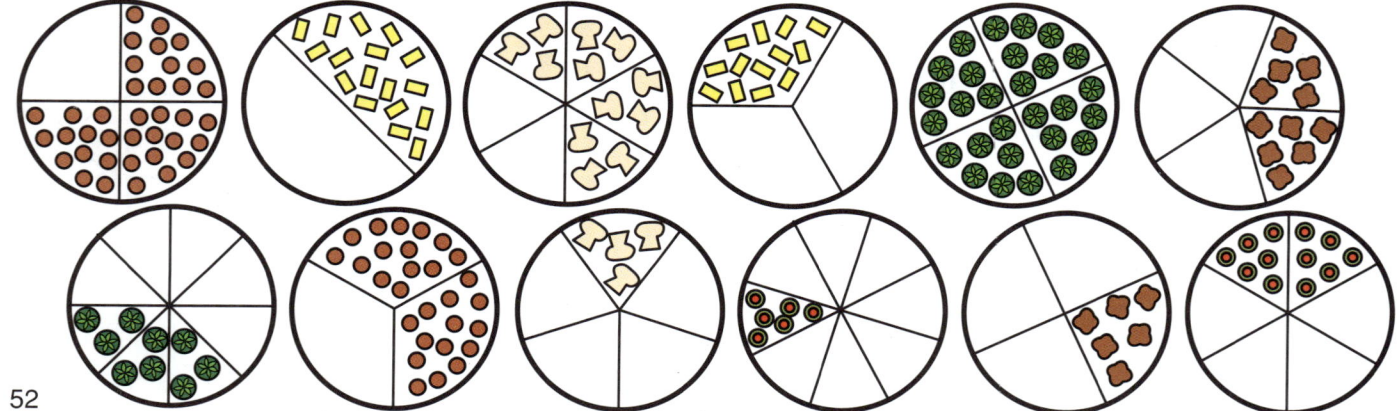

Name_____   Fractions: Parts of a group

Lunch at the Burger Palace

Read each problem.
Write a matching fraction
  beside each picture.
Two have been done for you.

1. Waitress Clara served 6 customers.
   3 people ordered burgers. $\frac{3}{6}$
   2 people ordered hot dogs.   _____
   1 person ordered fries.   _____

2. The Clark family had 4 burgers all together.
                                          _____
   Mrs. Clark and Darla had mustard on their burgers.
   Mr. Clark had ketchup on his. $\frac{1}{4}$
   Joey had cheese on his burger.   _____

3. Charlie cut his burger into 2 equal pieces.
   He ate 1 piece.   _____
   He gave 1 piece to his dog Buddy.   _____

4. John placed a take-out order for 3 burgers.
   He ordered 1 burger with mustard.   _____
   He ordered 2 burgers with ketchup.   _____

Name _____ Fractions: Parts of a set

Crunch the Numbers!

Pour $\frac{1}{2}$ cup of snack mix. Sort the snack mix by ingredient. Write a number to answer each question.
You will need snack mix with each ingredient below.

1. How many pieces of snack mix are pretzels? _____
2. How many pieces are cereal pieces? _____
3. How many pieces are crackers? _____
4. How many pieces do you have in all? _____

Use the information above.
Write a fraction to answer each question.

5. What part is pretzel?   6. What part is cereal?   7. What part is cracker?

On the lines, write a sentence comparing each ingredient.
(For example: I have more cereal than pretzels.)

8. Pretzel: _____

9. Cereal: _____

10. Cracker: _____

Now write a fraction to answer each question.

11. What part of your snack mix is pretzel and cereal? _____

12. What part is cereal and cracker? _____

13. What part is pretzel and cracker? _____

14. What part is not pretzel? _____

Name _____

Measurement

How Do Frogs and Toads Measure Up?

Frogs and toads come in many different sizes.
Read about each frog or toad.
Then find an item that is the same length.
Write the name of the item on the line.

The goliath frog is the largest of all frogs. This frog may grow to 12 inches long.	The paradoxical frog grows backwards! It shrinks from a large tadpole down to a 2-inch frog.	
The Cuban arrow-poison frog is the smallest of all frogs. This frog only grows to about $1/2$ inch long!	The chirping frog makes a sound like a cricket's chirp. This frog can grow to $1 1/2$ inches long.	Leopard frogs have many spots! They can grow to 4 inches long.
The giant toad is one of the largest toads! It can grow to 9 inches long.	Bullfrogs take about 5 years to become adults. These frogs can grow to 8 inches long.	Tree frogs are usually excellent jumpers. These tiny frogs only grow to about 1 inch long.
		The Surinam toad does not have a tongue! This unique toad can grow to 8 inches long.

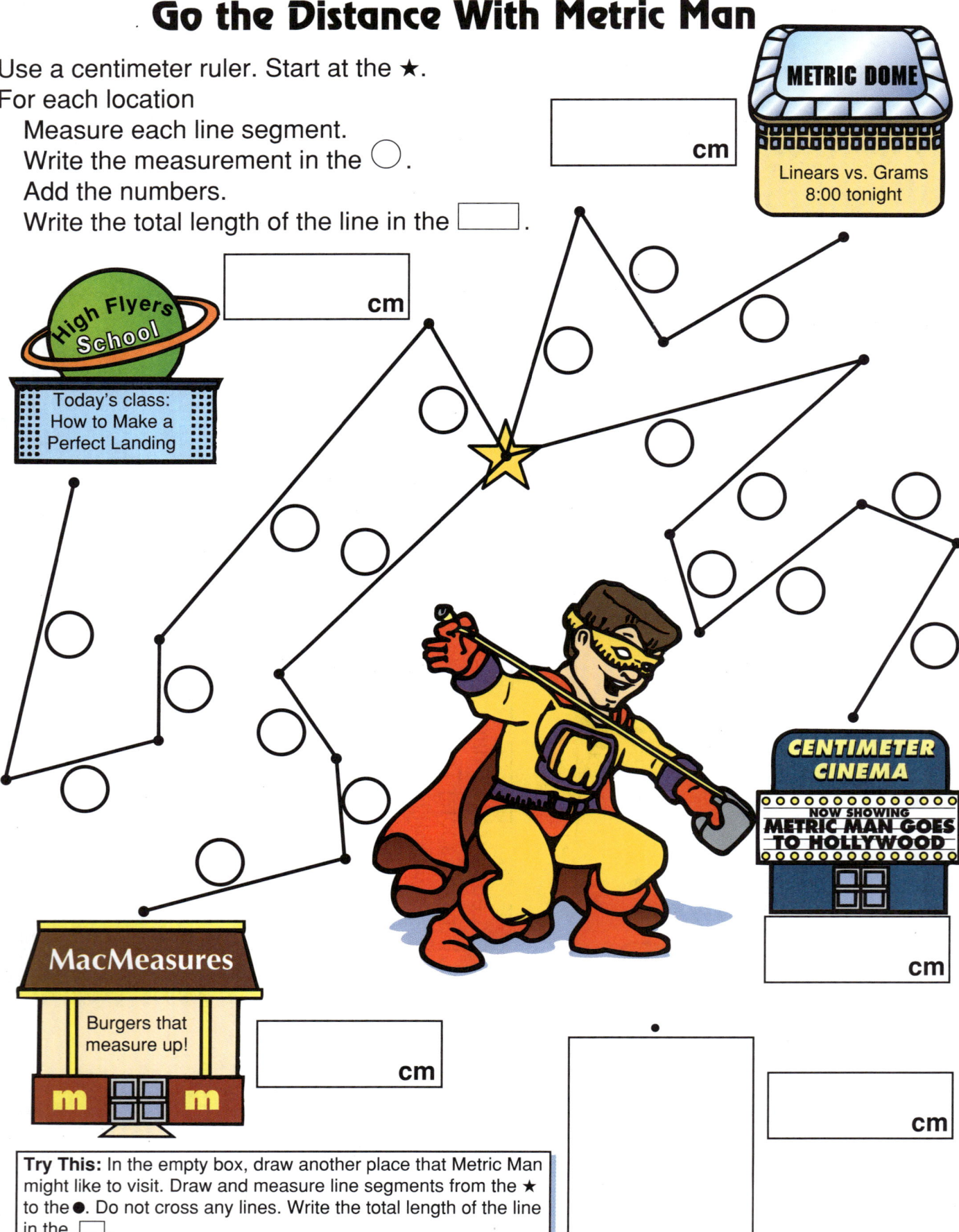

Name _____   Perimeter in centimeters

A Metric Masterpiece

Use a centimeter ruler.
Measure the perimeter of each shape.
Write your answers below.

Perimeter Color Code
0–11 cm = yellow
12–13 cm = red
14–16 cm = green
17–25 cm = purple

A. _____ cm
B. _____ cm
C. _____ cm
D. _____ cm
E. _____ cm
F. _____ cm
G. _____ cm
H. _____ cm
I. _____ cm
J. _____ cm

Name _____   Length: Finding perimeter

It's a Bird, It's a Plane...

Metric Man must patrol the perimeters of the parks in his precinct. Help him by finding the perimeter of each polygon.

At Home: Provide a centimeter ruler. Practice using a ruler with a leading edge.

Name _____ Area in square centimeters

Centimeter Caper

Metric Man is in the market for a magnificent new mantle (cape, that is). Count the squares to help him find the area of each cape.

SALE TODAY
Centimeter Checked Capes

FITTING ROOM
(SUPERHEROES ONLY)

A. _____ sq. cm

B. _____ sq. cm

C. _____ sq. cm

D. _____ sq. cm

E. _____ sq. cm

F. _____ sq. cm

G. _____ sq. cm

Name _____   Temperature: Compare Fahrenheit and Celsius

Whatever the Weather

Circle the most reasonable temperature estimate for each outdoor activity. Use the thermometer to help you.

1. Making snow angels —5°C 50°F

2. Collecting fall leaves 58°F 58°C

3. Planting a garden 10°C 65°F

4. Going to a football game 45°F 40°C

5. Surfing 60°C 90°F

6. Harvesting pumpkins 18°C 90°F

7. Watching the Independence Day parade 15°C 85°F

8. Dancing around a maypole 75°F 50°C

9. Eating a snow cone 37°C 50°F

10. Drinking hot chocolate 35°F 20°C

At Home: Keep an ongoing chart recording daily tempeatures in degrees Fahrenheit and Celsius.

Name _____   Capacity: Choosing appropriate measures

Bear-ly Measuring

Baby Bear is preparing Papa Bear's perfectly balanced porridge breakfast. Circle the correct measure for each item.

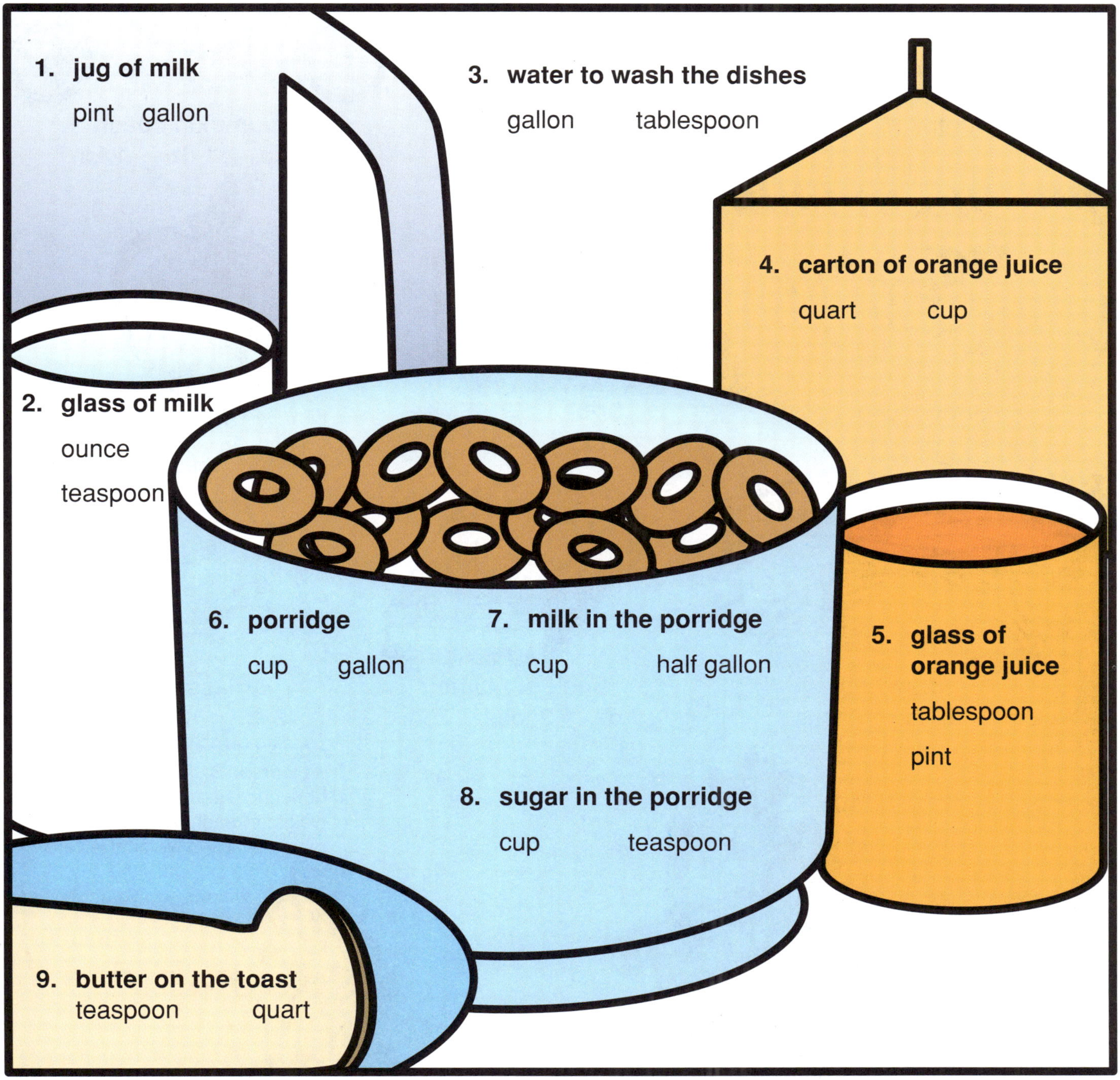

1. jug of milk
   pint   gallon

2. glass of milk
   ounce
   teaspoon

3. water to wash the dishes
   gallon   tablespoon

4. carton of orange juice
   quart   cup

5. glass of orange juice
   tablespoon
   pint

6. porridge
   cup   gallon

7. milk in the porridge
   cup   half gallon

8. sugar in the porridge
   cup   teaspoon

9. butter on the toast
   teaspoon   quart

At Home: Estimate the number of cups of cereal you eat or the gallons of milk your family drinks in a year.

Name _____ Weight: Estimation

Worth Its Weight in Gold

Circle the most likely estimate of the weight of each fairy-tale item.

1.
pumpkin
7 lb.   1 lb.   7 oz.

2.
crown
5 oz.   5 lb.   50 lb.

3.
pumpkin coach
1 lb.   1 oz.   1 ton

4.
magic beans
1 lb.   1 oz.   10 oz.

5.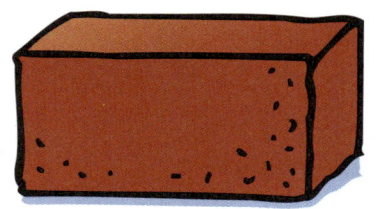
brick
1 lb.   1 oz.   10 lb.

6.
apple
3 lb.   6 oz.   16 oz.

7.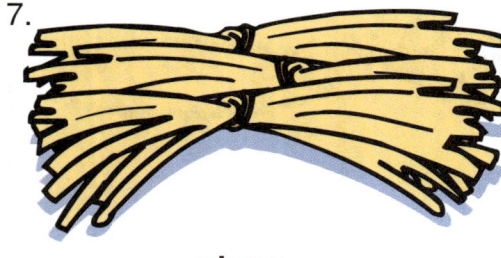
straw
2 lb.   20 lb.   2 tons

8.
book of magic
2 oz.   2 tons   2 lb.

9.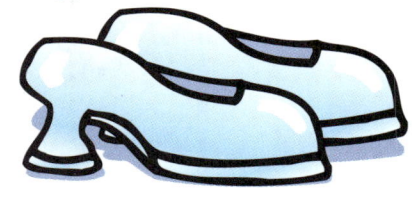
glass slippers
3 lb.   13 lb.   33 lb.

10.
throne
2 lb.   22 lb.   222 lb.

11. **At Home:** Gather several household items. Estimate the weight of each and record your estimate. Then weigh the item and compare the actual weight with your estimate. Keep practicing!

frog
1 lb.   1 oz.   1 ton

Name _____ Weight: Estimation

Heavy Thinking

Choose the most reasonable estimate for each item below. Order the estimates from least to greatest and write them on the blanks.

1.

Baby Bear	Mama Bear	Papa Bear
_____	_____	_____
200 lb.	110 lb.	10 lb.

2.

Little Billy Goat	Medium Billy Goat	Big Billy Goat
_____	_____	_____
15 kg	150 kg	50 kg

3.

Youngest Pig	Middle Pig	Oldest Pig
_____	_____	_____
40 kg	30 kg	10 lb.

4.

Elf Shoe	Glass Slipper	Woodsman's Boot
_____	_____	_____
1 lb.	8 oz.	5 kg

5.

Gumdrop	Candy Cane	Gingerbread Shingle
_____	_____	_____
2 lb.	2 g	2 oz.

6. Draw and compare three things from least to greatest. Label each with a reasonable estimate.

Name _____ Measurement: Review

For "Eggs-perts" Only

Fill in the blanks. Use the Color Code to color the eggs.

Color Code
If an egg shows a measure of
length, color the egg yellow
time, color the egg pink
liquid, color the egg green

a. 1 pint = _____ cups

b. 60 minutes = _____ hour

c. 1 quart = _____ cups

d. 1 yard = _____ feet

e. 1 gallon = _____ quarts

f. 6 feet = _____ yards

g. 1 year = _____ months

h. 1 foot = _____ inches

i. 1 day = _____ hours

j. 2 quarts = _____ pints

k. 1 week = _____ days

l. 1 yard = _____ inches

Third-Grade Parent Page

Time and Money

Time and money are important to your third grader, both academically and personally. Third graders are interested in when events occur and how long they last, how much items cost and how much change they should get.

Having learned to tell time to the quarter hour in second grade, third graders practice telling time in five-minute and one-minute increments on both digital and analog clocks. Make sure your child has opportunities to use both types of clocks at home.

Your child will use his estimation and problem-solving skills to solve word problems involving *elapsed time*. (For example, "The movie starts at 2:30 P.M. We get out of the show at 4:00 P.M. How long did the movie last?") He will gain proficiency in converting hours to minutes. He'll become familiar with A.M. and P.M. and routinely refer to a calendar.

Your child will work extensively with money in third grade. He'll again practice counting coin combinations to $1.00 and making change. Given the total cost and number of items, he'll be able to find the unit cost per item. He'll complete addition and subtraction of money with the decimal point and dollar sign. Problem solving this year will also include multiplying and dividing money amounts with decimals.

Your third grader should be able to
- read a calendar comparing periods of time such as 3 weeks to 19 days
- tell time to the minute
- solve problems involving elapsed time
- count coin combinations up to $1.00, starting with the coin with the greatest value
- make change from $1.00
- count coin combinations to make an amount with the fewest coins
- add and subtract money written with decimal point and dollar sign
- solve word problems involving money

Key Math Skills for Grade 3
Time and Money

- Time: telling time to the quarter hour
- Time: telling time to five minutes
- Time: telling time to the minute
- Time: determining elapsed time to solve word problems (for example, "The movie starts at 2:55. It is over at 4:15. How long is the show?")
- Money: counting combinations of coins to make an amount with the fewest coins
- Money: making change
- Money: solving word problems with money
- Money: adding and subtracting amounts with decimal notation

Name _____   Time to the quarter hour

Speedy Delivery

Write the time on the lines below each clock.
Find the matching time below. Color the box red.

   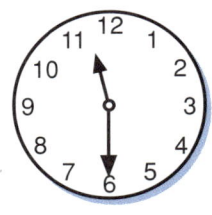 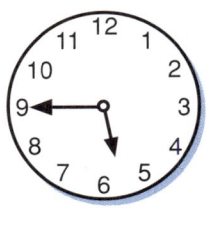

____ : ____   ____ : ____   ____ : ____   ____ : ____   ____ : ____

____ : ____   ____ : ____   ____ : ____   ____ : ____   ____ : ____

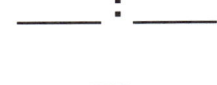  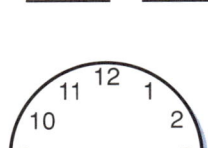  

   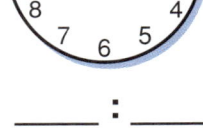

____ : ____   ____ : ____   ____ : ____   ____ : ____   ____ : ____

7:45	12:00	4:15	5:45	8:30
3:30				10:15
9:00				3:45
				6:30
1:15	6:00	9:45	11:30	2:00

Panda's Pizzeria

Bear in Mind—We Deliver on Time!

Name _____ Time to the quarter hour

Time for a Snack

Write the time on the lines below each clock.
Color the cheese holes yellow as you use the answers.

Name _____

Time: Word problems to five minutes

Perfect Timing

Read each problem.
Write the time on the lines.
Draw the hands on the clock to match.

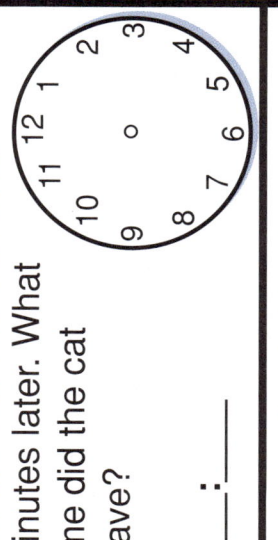
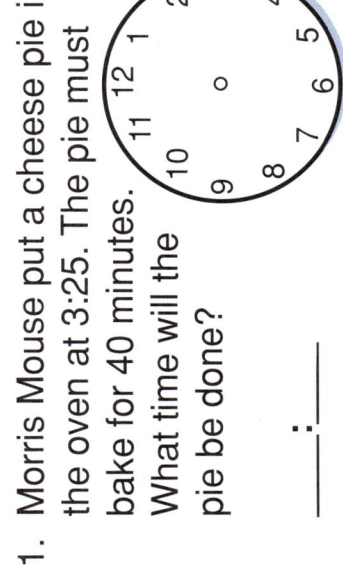

1. Morris Mouse put a cheese pie in the oven at 3:25. The pie must bake for 40 minutes. What time will the pie be done?

   __:__

2. Mia Mouse is going to visit Rita Rat. It takes 55 minutes to scurry to Rita's place. It is 8:20 now. What time will Mia get there?

   __:__

3. It was 11:55 when Marko Mouse saw the cat. The cat left 25 minutes later. What time did the cat leave?

   __:__

4. Mindy is expecting a visitor in a half hour. It is 9:10 now. If the visitor is on time, when will she arrive?

   __:__

5. It was 6:40 when Morris started feeling hungry. He didn't eat breakfast for 1 hour and 20 minutes. What time was breakfast?

   __:__

6. Marko called in his pizza order at 12:05. The pizza arrived 45 minutes later. What time was the pizza delivered?

   __:__

7. At 4:30 Mia started exercising. She worked out for one hour and five minutes. What time did she quit?

   __:__

8. Max is always 15 minutes late! The party started at 7:30. What time will Max get to the party?

   __:__

9. Morris just took a cheesecake out of the oven. It is 2:20. The cheesecake baked for 35 minutes. What time did Morris put the cake in the oven?

   __:__

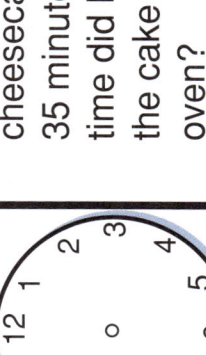

Name _____ Time to the minute

Every Minute Counts

Complete the hands on the clocks.
Write the letter of the correct clock by each sentence.

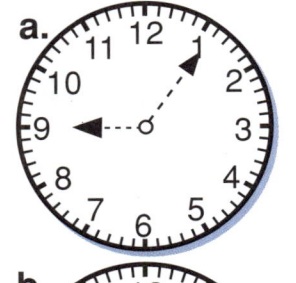

_____ Moe wakes up every morning at 6:37.

_____ At 7:22 he eats a bowl of Cheese Flakes for breakfast.

_____ The cat snoops around the front door at about 8:29.

_____ By 9:06 Moe has scurried off to Squeak School.

_____ Safety class begins at 10:43.

_____ When lunch is served at 11:55, he's very hungry.

_____ All the mice play until 12:12.

_____ School is out at 2:49.

_____ Moe meets his friends for a game of tag at 3:09.

_____ By 4:20 Moe is ready for a snack.

_____ Moe helps set the table for dinner at 5:38.

_____ By 7:39 Moe has finished his homework.

Try This: Estimate how many minutes it takes you to eat breakfast. Then time yourself!

Name _____ Time: Problem solving

Camp Ticktock

There is always something timely going on at Camp Ticktock. Use the schedule to help you solve the problems. You don't have a minute to lose. (Don't forget to write A.M. or P.M.)

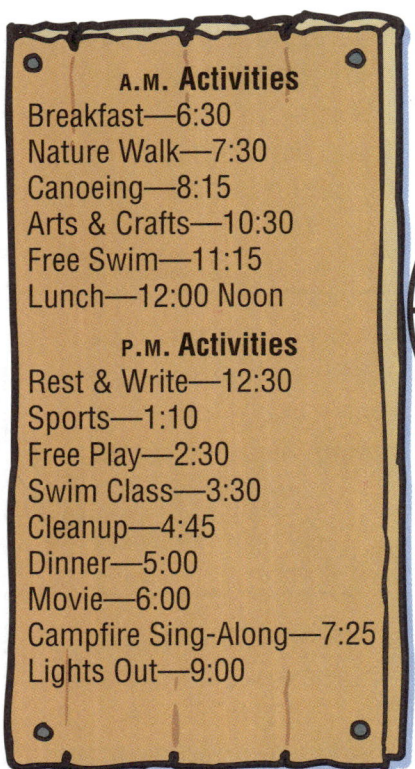

A.M. Activities
Breakfast—6:30
Nature Walk—7:30
Canoeing—8:15
Arts & Crafts—10:30
Free Swim—11:15
Lunch—12:00 Noon

P.M. Activities
Rest & Write—12:30
Sports—1:10
Free Play—2:30
Swim Class—3:30
Cleanup—4:45
Dinner—5:00
Movie—6:00
Campfire Sing-Along—7:25
Lights Out—9:00

Find each of the following events on the schedule. Draw the time on the clock.

1. Canoeing
2. Free Play
3. Movie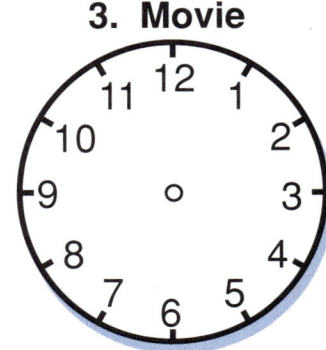

4. You arrive at lunch at 11:50 A.M. Are you early or late?

5. How much time can you spend at meals each day?

6. Is free swim in the morning or in the afternoon?

7. You arrive at camp in the afternoon when the clock looks like this: Where should you go?
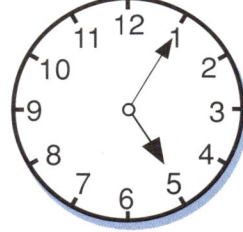

8. If it takes you 20 minutes to get ready for breakfast, what time should you wake up?

Write the following in numbers and words, and draw the hands on the clocks.

9. What time is 5 minutes after free swim begins?

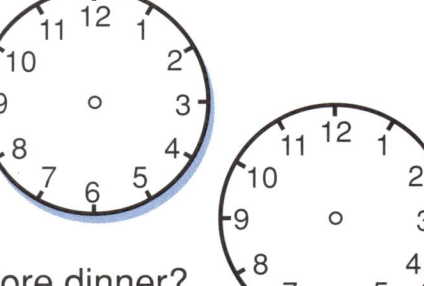

10. What time is 10 minutes before dinner?

Name_____   Time: Elapsed time problems

Camper Scamper

Use the schedule on page 72 to solve these problems, too!
Use the clocks to help you count the hours or minutes.

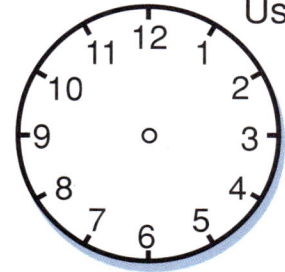

1. How much time is there between lights out and breakfast?

2. If it takes an hour to canoe across the lake and back, do you have time to do it twice in a session? Why or why not?

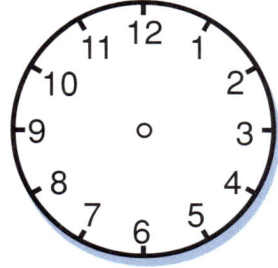

3. If you can hike a mile in 25 minutes, what time will it be after one mile of your nature walk?

4. How long can the movie be?

5. How much time can you spend in the water each day?

6. The sing-along lasts for an hour. What time does it end?

7. How much time will you then have to get ready for bed?

8. It takes you 10 minutes to walk to the pool and change for swim class. When should you leave to be ready on time?

9. If you finish lunch in 15 minutes, how much total time can you spend resting and writing?

10. Your home is located an hour and a half away from camp. If you leave at dinnertime, when will you get home?

Try This: Look in the newspaper for your favorite movie. How long is it between showings?

Name_____ Money: Counting on, decimal notation

Show Me the Money!

To add coins that are different, you can *count on*.
Here's an example:

    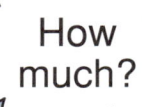

- First, you have to arrange the coins from greatest to least value.
- Then you can count on like this:

25¢   **35¢**   **40¢**   **45¢**

Another way to say 45 cents is to write 45 with a cents sign like this: 45¢.

You do not need a cents sign if you use a dollar sign ($) and a decimal point like this: $0.45.

There may be more than one way to make 45 cents.

Write these money amounts with a dollar sign and decimal point.

1. 55 cents ____.____

2. 75 cents ____.____

3. one dollar and ten cents ____.____

4. two dollars and no cents ____.____

5. five dollars ____.____

6. 24 dollars and 25 cents ____.____

7. eighteen dollars and sixty cents ____.____

8. twenty-two dollars and twenty-two cents ____.____

9. seven dollars and ninety-nine cents ____.____

10. five cents ($5/100$ of a dollar) ____.____

Name _____ Money: Making change

Penelope's Pig Emporium

Write the amount of money you have in the blank.
Subtract the cost of the item you buy.
Color the amount of money you have left.

Money You Have	You Buy	Money You Have Left
(quarter, dime, nickel, nickel) ____¢	Slop Savers 25¢	(dime, dime, nickel, penny, penny)
(quarter, quarter, dime, dime, nickel) ____¢	Pretty Piggy 72¢ Tail Curler	(dime, penny, nickel, nickel, nickel)
(quarter, dime, dime, dime, nickel) ____¢	55¢ a tube deep-heating "Oink-ment"	(quarter, dime, nickel, nickel, penny)
(dime, dime, nickel, penny, dime, dime, nickel, penny) ____¢	Corn Meal 40¢	(dime, dime, dime, dime, penny, penny)
(quarter, quarter, dime) ____¢	Hoof Shine 34¢	(dime, dime, nickel, penny, penny, penny)
(quarter, quarter, quarter) ____¢	Mud Pack 67¢	(dime, nickel, nickel, nickel, penny)
(quarter, nickel, penny, penny, penny, dime) ____¢	Soap 18¢ PIG-B-NEAT	(dime, nickel, nickel, nickel, penny, penny)

75

Name _____   Three-digit addition, no regrouping

Silly Sandwich Shop

Read the menu. Find the total cost of each silly sandwich order.

Today's Menu

Type of sandwich
- sub, hero, hoagie, poor boy, torpedo .... $ 2.00
- pita, club, open face .... $ 3.00

Sandwich Stuffers
- tuna fish .... 33¢
- banana .... 32¢
- peanut butter .... 30¢
- jelly .... 34¢
- cheese .... 31¢
- dill pickle .... 25¢

Sandwich Spreads
- marshmallow creme .... 20¢
- barbecue sauce .... 12¢
- hot fudge .... 16¢
- mustard .... 10¢
- catsup .... 10¢
- whipped cream .... 14¢

Order #1
club	.
jelly	.
cheese	.
catsup	.
Total	$.

Order #2
poor boy	.
peanut butter	.
dill pickle	.
barbecue sauce	.
Total	$.

Order #3
open face	.
banana	.
mustard	.
hot fudge	.
Total	$.

Order #4
torpedo	.
tuna fish	.
jelly	.
marshmallow creme	.
Total	$.

Order #5
hoagie	.
cheese	.
barbecue sauce	.
dill pickle	.
Total	$.

Order #6
pita	.
peanut butter	.
whipped cream	.
catsup	.
Total	$.

Name_____ Money: Word problems

Uncle Sam's Shopping

Study the items in the Campaign Store.
Read each problem.
Solve the problem in its box.
Write the answer in the blank star beside it.

Campaign Store

| $0.55 button | $0.69 bumper sticker | $0.75 key chain | $0.85 poster | $0.95 hat | $1.10 flag | $1.50 box of pencils | $1.75 bunch of balloons |

1. Ann bought a bunch of balloons and a key chain. How much money did she spend?

2. Thomas wants to buy two buttons. He has $1.00. How much more money does he need?

3. How much more than a bumper sticker does a poster cost?

4. Jack bought a hat and a button. He gave the clerk $2.00. How much change should he get?

5. Samantha wants to buy two boxes of pencils. How much money does she need?

6. Alex bought a flag and a hat. Then he bought a poster. How much did he spend in all?

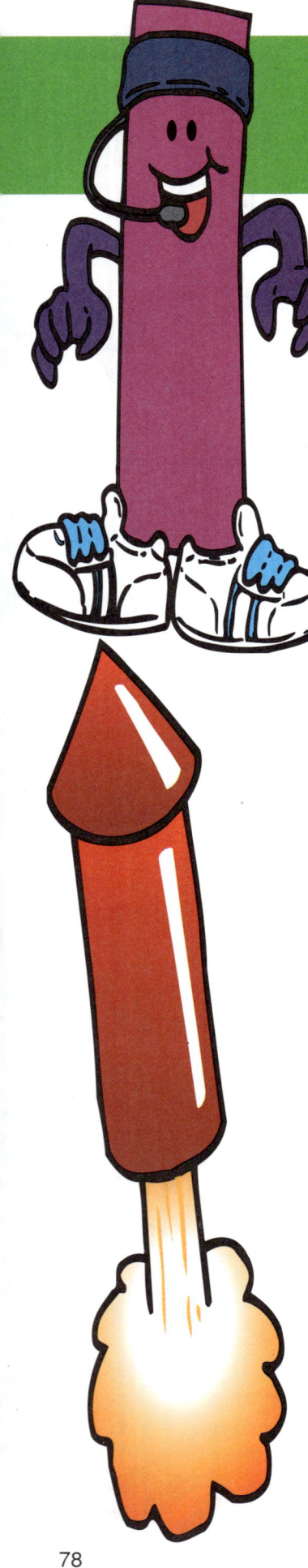

Third-Grade Parent Page

Geometry

In third grade, your child will further explore geometric shapes and the results of moving, flipping, or turning shapes. He'll be able to describe and compare both two-dimensional and three-dimensional figures. He'll learn to describe locations using *coordinate geometry*, or points on a grid. He'll be asked to identify the following, all of which are defined and illustrated for you on the pages that follow:

- lines, rays, and *line segments*
- angles greater and less than a *right angle*
- kinds of polygons including *triangles, quadrilaterals, pentagons, hexagons, and octagons*
- three-dimensional figures including *pyramids, spheres, cylinders, cones, cubes, and triangular, rectangular, and square prisms*
- *congruent* shapes (figures having the same size and shape)
- *similar* shapes (same in shape but different in size)
- *lines of symmetry* (made by folding along a line so that two parts match exactly)
- *transformations* (made by turning, sliding, or flipping the position of a figure)

Every day, help your child see geometric shapes in art, architecture, and in his environment. For example, you can bend straws to show angles while you are waiting for your meal in a restaurant. You can play a solid-figure version of I Spy in the supermarket. Say, "I spy a cylinder!" and see if your child can too. If your child is familiar with geometry vocabulary and concepts, he will be more comfortable using his knowledge to solve problems.

Third graders should be able to
- identify and compare *plane* (two-dimensional) and *solid* (three-dimensional) geometric shapes
- compare and sort solid figures, counting the number of *faces* or edges
- draw one or more lines of symmetry
- identify and combine congruent figures
- locate points on a grid
- recognize and apply transformations (flipping, sliding, or turning shapes)
- recognize geometric shapes and structures in the environment

Key Math Skills for Grade 3
Geometry

- Plane figures: identifying, comparing, and sorting polygons—*triangles, quadrilaterals, pentagons, hexagons,* and *octagons*
- Solid figures: identifying, comparing, and sorting solid shapes—such as spheres, cubes, cylinders, pyramids, and rectangular prisms—according to number of faces, edges, or *vertices*
- Combining and taking apart shapes (for example, separating and combining shapes to make new figures using *tangrams*)
- Identifying *congruent* figures (for example, arranging two congruent triangles to form a rectangle)
- Identifying and creating *lines of symmetry*
- Recognizing and applying *slides, flips,* and *turns*
- Recognizing shapes from different perspectives
- Recognizing geometric shapes and structures in the environment

Box It Up
Different sizes and shapes of boxes and containers are terrific for showing the relationship between two- and three-dimensional figures. Help your child carefully cut the boxes along the edges. Try to keep the cardboard attached in one piece when flattened. Then talk about relative size, shape, right angles, faces, and edges. Compare how much the boxes hold with the size of the flattened boxes and relate this to volume with area and perimeter.

Art Smart
Check out a local art museum—the more modern, the better. There are lots of geometric designs in patterns in art. Walk or drive through any neighborhood to find shapes in the architecture of the buildings. Encourage your child to identify, classify, and describe them. Take photographs of some favorites, and use permanent marker to accent the shapes you found. Then glue the photos on poster board to make a collage.

Geometric Geography
Join your child in tracing possible routes on street maps. Include vocabulary words like *intersecting, perpendicular,* and *parallel* as you do. Then create a map of your own design: a room in your home, your town, or an imaginary place.

Getting Into Shapes

Give your youngster a whole new angle on polygons with this hands-on activity.

1. Have your child cut out her four triangles along the bold lines.
2. Tell your child that to complete "Getting Into Shapes" she will have to use the triangle patterns to form different polygons. Tell her to use the triangle rule when forming polygons. Then explain and model the triangle rule shown on this page.
3. If desired, your child can store her triangles in a resealable plastic bag. Encourage her to find various ways to make triangles, quadrilaterals, pentagons, and hexagons using all four triangles.

Triangle Rule
When making polygons, put the triangles together so that the adjacent sides are the same length and match exactly.

These are okay.

These are not okay.

Triangle Patterns
See page 81 for how to use these patterns.

Name _____ Geometry: Identifying and constructing polygons

Getting Into Shapes

Use the word bank to label each set of polygons.
Tell how many sides and angles each polygon type has.
Use your triangles to make the different polygon types.
Draw your answer in each box.
The first one is done for you.

Remember the triangle rule!

Word Bank
hexagons   quadrilaterals
pentagons   triangles

Polygons	How can a polygon of this type be made…	How can a polygon of this type be made…
A. _____ ___ sides ___ angles	with 2 triangles?	with 4 triangles?
B. _____ ___ sides ___ angles	with 2 triangles?	with 4 triangles?
C. _____ ___ sides ___ angles	with 3 triangles?	with 4 triangles?
D. _____ ___ sides ___ angles	with 4 triangles?	a different way with 4 triangles?

At Home: Provide practice with geometry vocabulary. Ask, "Which group of polygons would have more sides—2 triangles and 1 quadrilateral or 1 hexagon and 1 pentagon?"

Name _____

Geometry: Identify lines, line segments, and rays

Lining Up Fireworks

A **line** is straight and continues on in both directions. ↔

A **line segment** has a point at each end. It is part of a line. •—•

A **ray** is also part of a line. It continues on in one direction and has a point at the other end. •→

Label each line, line segment, and ray.

Draw a line.

Draw a line segment.

Draw a ray.

Name _____   Geometry: Identify and categorize angles

Quilt Quest

An angle is formed when two rays meet at a point.
Right angles form square corners.

**Some angles are greater than right angles,
and some angles are less than right angles.**

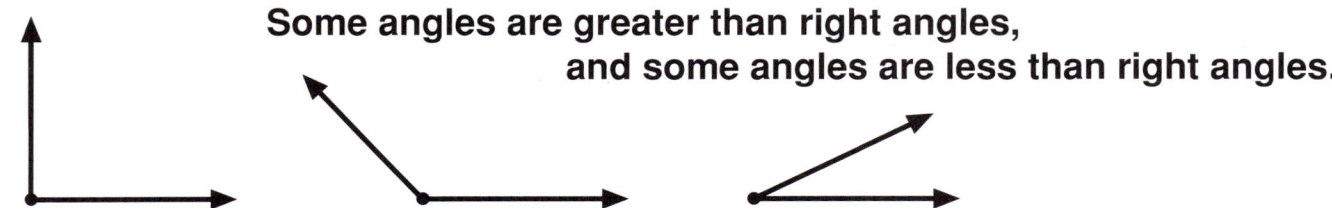

Next to each angle in the quilt squares below, write *right, greater,* or *less* to name the angle.

"The Pinwheel"

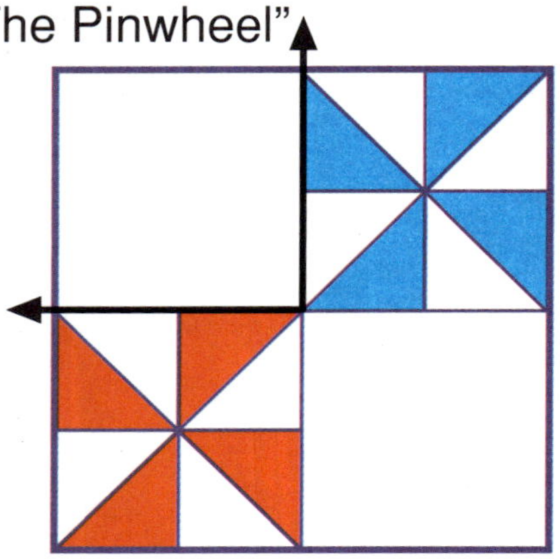

1. _____

"Flags"

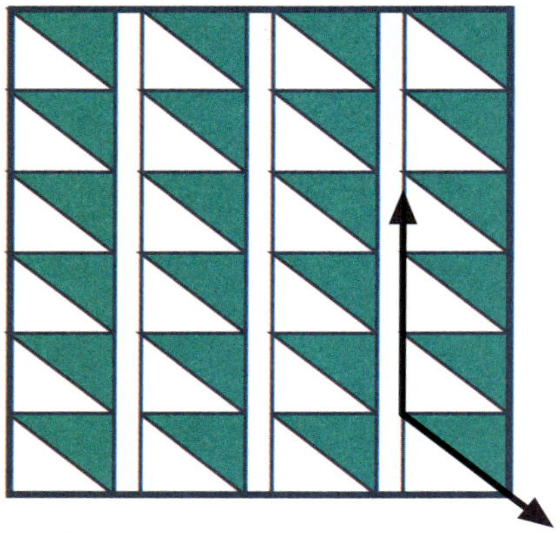

2. _____

"Flying Geese"

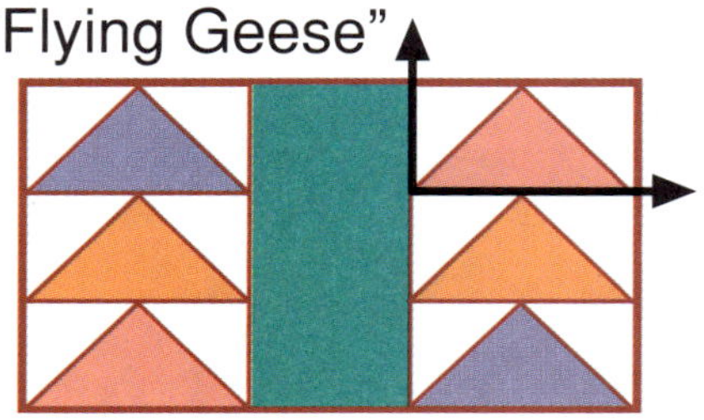

3. _____

"The Milky Way"

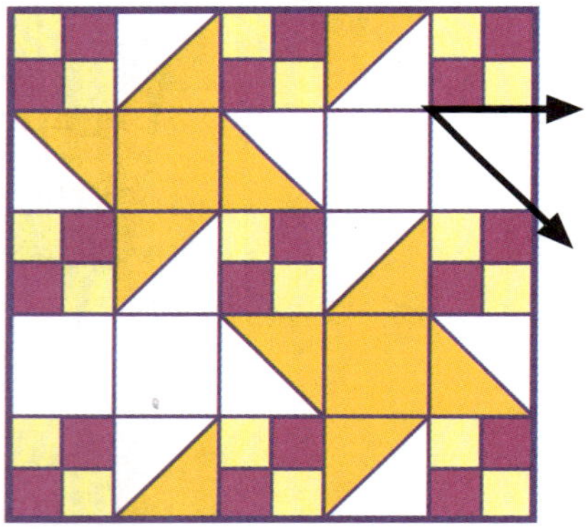

4. _____

"The Saw Tooth Star"

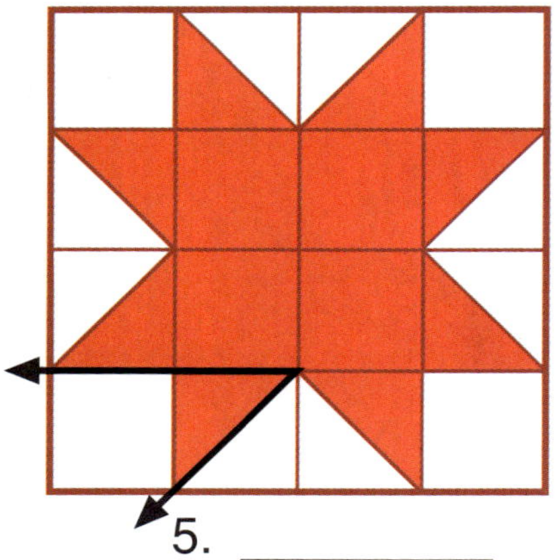

5. _____

"The Pine Tree"

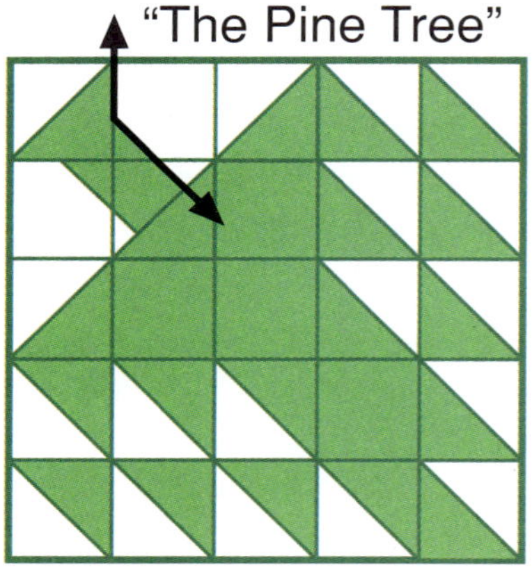

6. _____

In the space to the right, draw a right angle, an angle greater than a right angle, and an angle less than a right angle.

Try This: Fit a corner of a piece of paper into angles to help identify them.

Name _____ Geometry: Identify and create lines of symmetry

Symmetry Quilts

Many quilt squares have lines of symmetry, which can be horizontal, vertical, or diagonal. If you divide a figure in half at a line of symmetry, the sides are mirror images.

Draw the line or lines of symmetry on each quilt square.
Hint: If you fold a figure on a line of symmetry, the sides will match.

"The Churn Dash" has <u>0</u> lines of symmetry.

"The Maple Leaf" has <u>1</u> line of symmetry.

"The Road to Oklahoma" has <u>2</u> lines of symmetry.

"The 9 Patch Star" has <u>4</u> lines of symmetry.

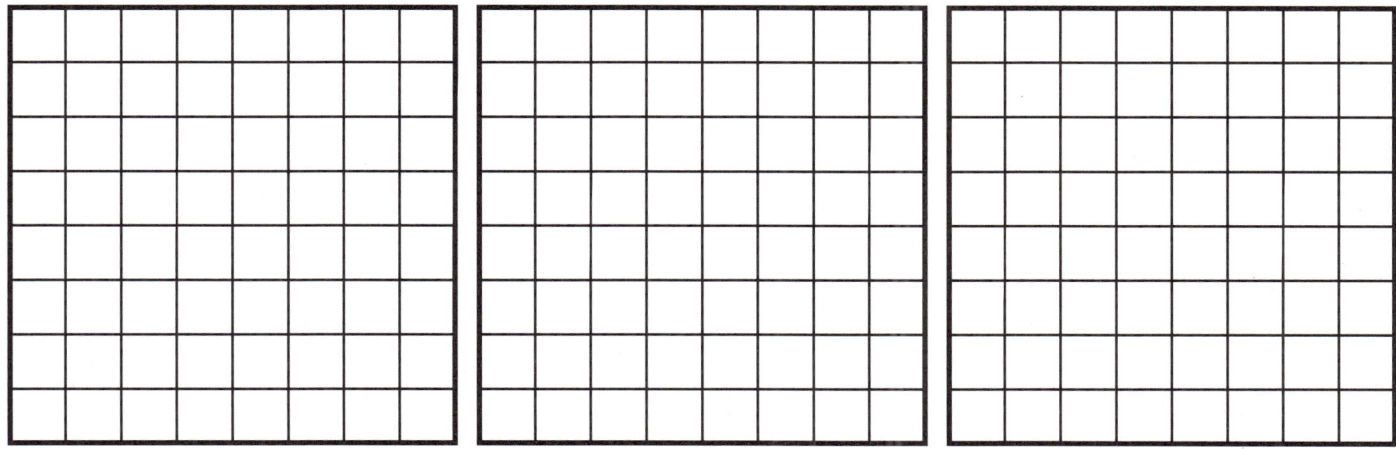

Now use the grids below to design quilt squares of your own with different numbers of lines of symmetry. (Do this in pencil first.)
Write the number of lines of symmetry under each one.

_____   _____   _____

At Home: Check any patchwork items at your house for lines of symmetry.

Name _____   Perform slides, flips, turns

Transformation Trapeze

These fabulous flying figures flip and turn on the trusty trapeze. These moves are called **transformations**.
On each blank line, draw the transformation.

Flip—flip over the dotted line   Slide—slide right, up, down   Turn—turn on one point

1.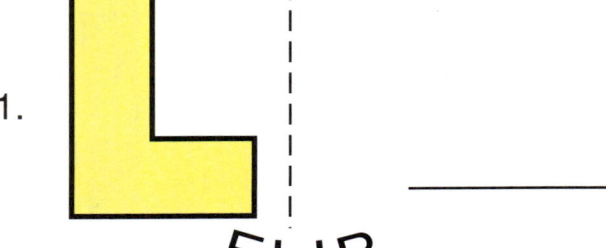
FLIP

5.
SLIDE

2.
TURN

6.
FLIP

3.
SLIDE

7.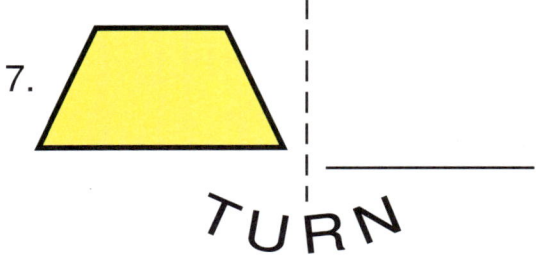
TURN

4.
FLIP

8.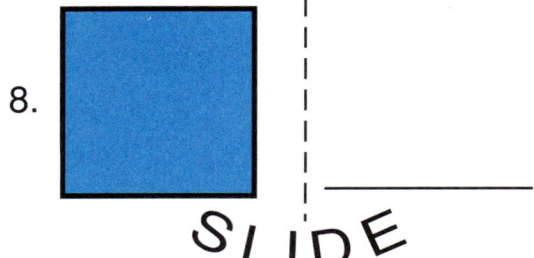
SLIDE

86   ©The Education Center, Inc. • Learning Library® • TEC3719

Third-Grade Parent Page
Patterns, Functions, and Algebra

Algebra in third grade? No problem! This year your child will learn to fill in the blanks in math equations. He'll be able to find missing *addends* by analyzing related facts. For example, if $6 + 5 = 11$, then in $5 + x = 11$, $x = 6$. He will also find missing operations in problems like $4 \_\_ 2 = 8$. He will form and write simple equations related to problem solving. *Inequalities* and *variables* (unknowns identified by letters or symbols) will be added to the equations.

The process begins with simple number patterns: recognizing, describing, and extending them. Your child will use his number sense, basic facts, and knowledge of even and odd. He'll learn to find the rule, a gamelike process that many children really enjoy.

He will perform measurement conversions, like $\_\_$ inches = $\_\_$ feet x 12, and total cost given the cost per unit.

Your child will also learn to use a grid system and *coordinates* to describe relationships, locations, and movement. When your child learns the order of coordinate pairs, (over to a friend's house, then up the steps), problem solving will be easier.

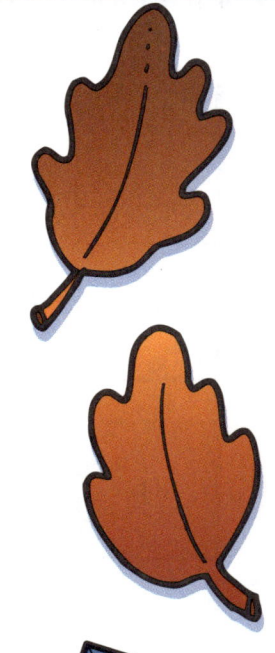

Key Math Skills for Grade 3
Patterns, Functions, and Algebra

- Can describe and extend geometric and number patterns
- Can represent patterns and functions using words, tables, and graphs Uses graphs, tables, and equations to draw conclusions
- Can represent math situations using symbols and equations
- Can select the operation to make an equation true (for example, $4 \_\_ 3 = 12$. What operational symbol goes in the blank?)
- Can represent a *variable* as an unknown using a letter or symbol
- Expresses math relationships with equations (for example, $\_\_$ inches = $\_\_$ feet x 12)
- Finds the cost of multiple items given the cost per unit
- Investigates how a change in one variable relates to a change in a second variable

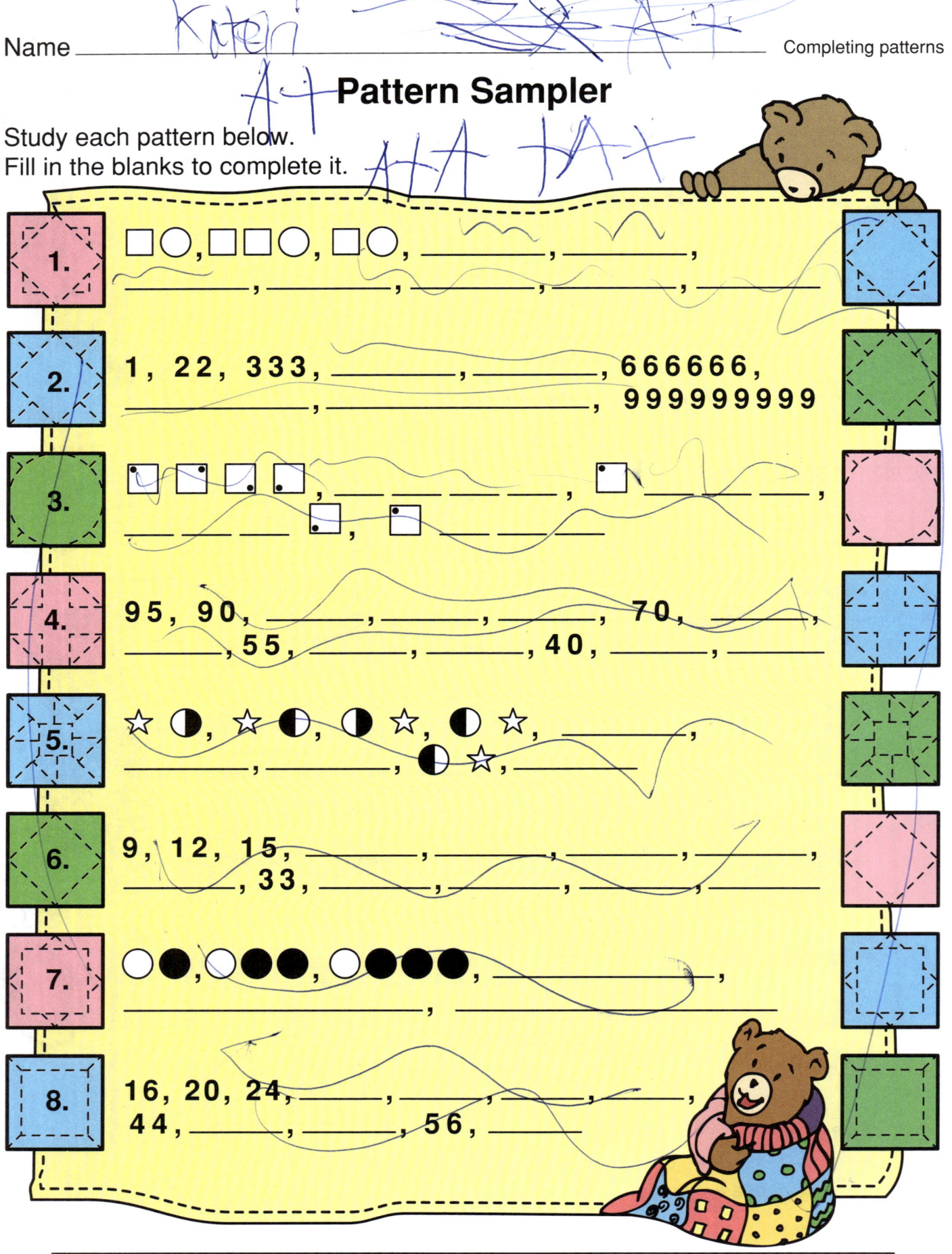

Name _____   Number patterns: Even, odd

Pattern Cross-Stitch

Fill in the blanks to complete each pattern.

1. 3, 5, 7, 9, ___, ___
2. 4, 6, 8, ___, 12, ___
3. 45, ___, 35, 30, ___, ___
4. 0, 1, 0, ___, 0, 3
5. 22, ___, 18, 16, ___, ___
6. 33, 35, ___, ___, 41, 43, ___
7. 1, 2, 4, 8, 16, ___
8. 31, 41, ___, ___, 71, ___
9. 50, 54, 58, ___, ___, ___

10. Make a pattern of your own.

At Home: Use beans, shells, candy, beads, cereal, or any other small objects to make a pattern. Challenge your child to make a number pattern that is similar to it. Switch roles the next day, and include other family members, too!

Name _____   Functions: Find the rule

"Spook-tacular" Secrets

Look at each table.
Fill in each empty box with a number or a secret rule.

1.

Rule: Add 9			
2	6	8	4

4.

Rule: Double the number			
2	6	8	10

2.

Rule: Subtract 7			
15	13	17	11

5.

Rule: Multiply by 5			
1	8	4	5

3.

Rule:			
14	9	46	13
24	19	56	23

6.

Rule:			
15	17	13	18
9		7	

90   ©The Education Center, Inc. • Learning Library® • TEC3719

Name _____   Math functions: Finding missing factors

Fall Fest Factors

Find the missing factors to solve these story problems.
The first one is started for you.

1. You are making Fall Festival party bags. You want to put 2 prizes in each bag. How many bags can you make if you have 22 prizes?

   2 x _____ = 22

2. 8 trick-or-treaters come to your candy booth. If you give out 32 pieces of candy, how many does each child get?

   _____ x _____ = _____

3. Your favorite fall song plays 6 times every hour. If you hear it 24 times in all, how many hours were you there?

   _____ x _____ = _____

4. You and 4 friends are at the dunking booth. If the 5 of you threw 20 balls all together, how many did each of you throw?

   _____ x _____ = _____

5. You threw 10 rings at the ring toss game. If you spent $1.50, how much did each ring cost?

   _____ x _____ = _____

6. You won the same number of prizes at miniature golf, balloon popping, and the sack race. If you won a total of 21 prizes, how many prizes did you win at each game?

   _____ x _____ = _____

More Practice:

7. 4 x _____ = 0   8. _____ x 6 = 36   9. _____ x 7 = 7

10. 9 x _____ = 72   11. _____ x 2 = 18   12. 3 x _____ = 9

Names _____   Algebra: Writing equations

The Big Cheese

Begin at a space marked "Start." Follow the game rules below.
Circle each numeral as you climb the mountain.
Then, on another sheet of paper, write and solve an equation for the path you took.
The highest answer wins.

Game Rules	1. Follow the lines. 2. Do not move backwards. 3. Each space can be used only once unless it is starred.

Name _____ Algebra: Writing equations, using a calculator

Cosmic Calculations

Use a calculator to solve each problem. Write the answer on the planet at the end of the problem.

*Remember, press **clear** before you start a new row!*

Start ... **Finish**

1. 5 + 2 = − 3 = × 4 =

2. 6 × 3 = + 5 = − 4 =

3. 9 − 4 = × 6 =

4. 8 × 4 = × 3 = − 4 =

5. 7 + 8 = × 3 = − 4 =

6. 3 × 7 = + 9 = × 2 =

Try This: Here's a cosmic challenge! Write +, −, or × to complete these problems. Use a calculator to help you.

6 ☐ 6 ☐ 6 = 42   9 ☐ 5 ☐ 7 = 52

Name _____ Ordered pairs, map coordinates

A Gem of a Map!

Matt Miner buried his gems at a secret location.
Cut and paste the gems.

Gem Map

	A	B	C	D
6				
5				
4				
3				
2				
1				

Code
- amber = D3
- amethysts = A6
- diamonds = B4
- emeralds = C1
- gold = A2
- morganite = C5
- onyx = D6
- rubies = B3
- sapphires = A1
- topaz = D5

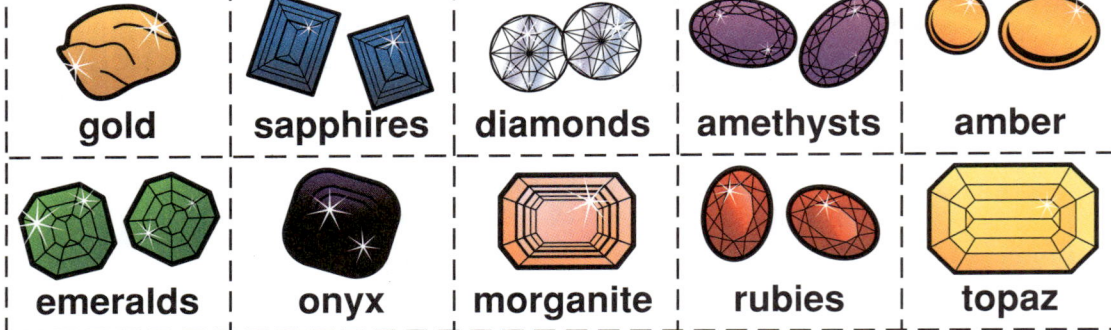

gold · sapphires · diamonds · amethysts · amber
emeralds · onyx · morganite · rubies · topaz

94

Name _____ Ordered pairs

Coins of the World

Sure you're familiar with the U.S. coins, but how about coins from around the world? The names of other countries' coins are hidden in the grid below. To discover the names of these coins, write the letter for each ordered pair of numbers in the blanks below. The first one has been started for you.

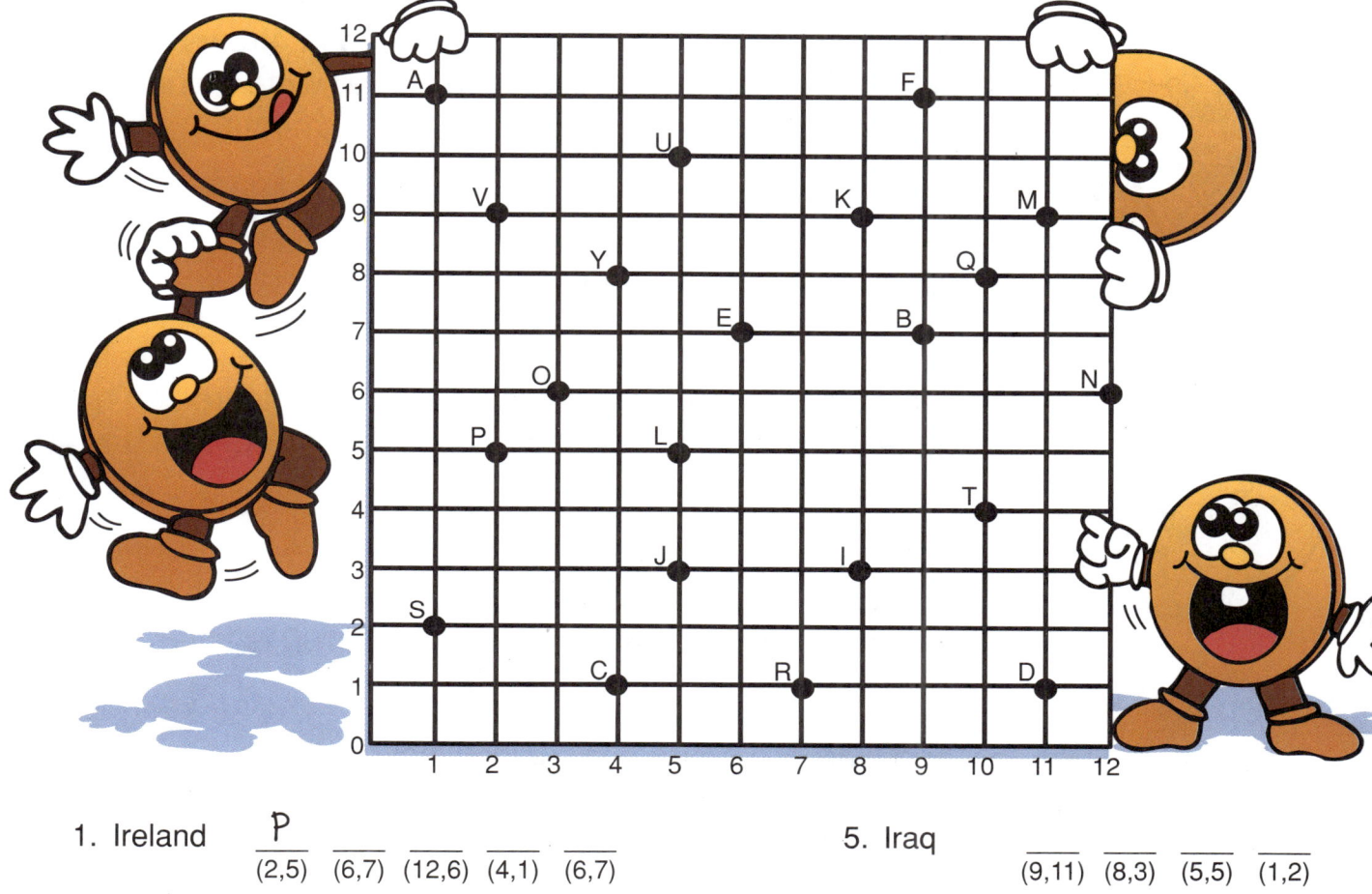

1. Ireland $\underline{P}$ $\underline{}$ $\underline{}$ $\underline{}$ $\underline{}$
   (2,5) (6,7) (12,6) (4,1) (6,7)

2. Mexico $\underline{}$ $\underline{}$ $\underline{}$ $\underline{}$
   (2,5) (6,7) (1,2) (3,6)

3. Belgium $\underline{}$ $\underline{}$ $\underline{}$ $\underline{}$ $\underline{}$
   (9,11) (7,1) (1,11) (12,6) (4,1)

4. Argentina $\underline{}$ $\underline{}$ $\underline{}$ $\underline{}$ $\underline{}$ $\underline{}$ $\underline{}$
   (4,1) (6,7) (12,6) (10,4) (1,11) (2,9) (3,6)

5. Iraq $\underline{}$ $\underline{}$ $\underline{}$ $\underline{}$
   (9,11) (8,3) (5,5) (1,2)

6. Japan $\underline{}$ $\underline{}$ $\underline{}$
   (4,8) (6,7) (12,6)

7. Italy $\underline{}$ $\underline{}$ $\underline{}$ $\underline{}$
   (5,5) (8,3) (7,1) (1,11)

8. Nigeria $\underline{}$ $\underline{}$ $\underline{}$ $\underline{}$
   (8,9) (3,6) (9,7) (3,6)

Use the grid to write the ordered pairs of numbers for the U.S. coins named below.

1. quarter ___ ___ ___ ___ ___ ___ ___
2. dime ___ ___ ___ ___
3. nickel ___ ___ ___ ___ ___ ___
4. penny ___ ___ ___ ___ ___

At Home: Choose a simple page from a coloring book. Make a copy of it. Draw one-inch grid lines on the copy. Label the back of each square with its coordinates, and cut the squares apart. Make a blank grid with your child. Give your child one square at a time and challenge him to place it on the grid correctly. Repeat until the image is complete.

Name_____   Algebra: Word problems

Collectors' Corner

Solve the problems and answer the questions.
Use number sentences, drawings, and patterns to help you.

1. Sam has his poster collection arranged in 4 rows with 3 posters in each row. Draw an array and write a number sentence to show how many posters Sam has.

2. Jen spent $5 on each one of her model planes. How many did she buy if she spent $35 in all?

3. Jim collects postcards, and he can fit 4 postcards on a page in his album. How many pages are filled if he has 40 postcards?

4. Lee's trading cards have only odd numbers. If she has #91 and #97, which cards between 90 and 100 is she missing?

5. Ann wants to share her shell collection. If she gives away 64 shells, an equal number to each of 8 friends, how many shells will each friend get?

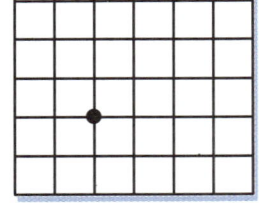

6. Joe buried his coin collection in his backyard. What coordinate pair shows the location of the treasure?

7. Sal needs 16 more stamps to complete his first album. How many stamps does he have if the album holds 50 stamps?

8. Kay got 2 state quarters a day for a week. Jay got one each day for 3 weeks. Write a number sentence to show who has more quarters.

Name _____   Geometry, patterns, and algebra review

Quiz Show

Circle the letter of the correct answer for each problem.
How much $$ can you win?

	GEOMETRY	PATTERNS	ALGEBRA
$100	1. Which will not roll? a) sphere b) cylinder c) cone d) pyramid	2. Which numbers complete the pattern? 3, 6, 9, __, __, __ a) 12, 15, 18 b) 10, 11, 12 c) 10, 12, 14 d) 10, 13, 16	3. What goes in the box? 4 ☐ 2 = 8 a) + b) = c) 6 d) x
$200	4. Which has a right angle? a) square b) pentagon c) hexagon d) circle	5. Which rule fits the pattern? 30, 25, 20, 15, 10 a) add 5 b) subtract 5 c) multiply by 5 d) divide by 5	6. What is the value of c in $c - 5 = 7$? a) 19 b) 12 c) 2 d) 0
$300	7. Which is a ray? a) ↕ b) •—• c) ↓ d) ↗	8. What will be the seventh number in this pattern? 2, 4, 6, 8 a) 14 b) 10 c) 4 d) 9	9. Which of the following are true? a) 2 + 6 = 8 + 2 b) 2 + 6 = 26 c) 2 + 6 = 8 d) 2 + 6 = 6 + 2

DOUBLE BONUS!!

10. What goes in the blank?
    3 x 8 ___ 20
    a) =   b) 24   c) <   d) >

11. Which has more than one line of symmetry?
    a) T   b) ▢   c) ▲   d) ♥

Name_____   Geometry, patterns, and algebra review

Grab Bags

Circle the correct answer for each problem.

1. What goes in the box?

   45 □ 9 = 5

   a) +   b) −
   c) ×   d) ÷

2. Which equation fits the story? Maya has 6 dolls. How many more does she need to have a dozen?

   a) 1 dozen = 12   b) 6 + 12 = ___
   c) 6 = 12   d) 6 + ___ = 12

3. Which of the following is *not* true?

   a) 2 × 5 = 10
   b) 4 × 2 = 2 + 2 + 2 + 2
   c) 2 × 5 > 5 × 2
   d) 2 × 4 = 4 × 2

4. Which of the following does not belong?

   a) sphere   b) rectangle
   c) circle   d) triangle

5. I have 6 faces, 12 edges, and 8 corners. What am I?

   a) square
   b) rectangular prism
   c) rectangle   d) pyramid

6. Which ordered pair shows the location of the triangle?

   a) (2, 3)
   b) (4, 1)
   c) (1, 4)
   d) (3, 2)

7. What is the missing factor?

   ___ × 4 = 36

   a) 9   b) 40   c) 42   d) 4

8. Which number sequence describes the array?

   a) 4 + 3 = 7   b) 4 + 3 = 12
   c) 2 × 6 = 12   d) 4 × 3 = 12

9. What goes in the box?

   $\frac{1}{2} = \frac{\square}{12}$

   a) 2   b) 6
   c) 24   d) 1

10. What number will be on the tenth bead?

    a) 1   b) 5   c) 6   d) 10

Third-Grade Parent Page

Graphing and Probability

Graphing and probability are emphasized in third-grade math, in part because graphs are used in the science and social studies content areas. It is likely your child will graph everything from favorite ice-cream flavors to rates of plant growth.

Your third grader will begin by asking questions that she can answer by gathering information. Then she'll design an investigation to answer the questions. She might use observations, surveys, or an experiment to collect data. She'll choose the best way to display this information from a variety of graphs, charts, or tables. Then she'll read the graphs or charts to compare data, make predictions, and draw conclusions. In summary, your child will learn how to
- take a survey to gather data
- record data using tally marks
- organize and display information in a graph or chart
- draw conclusions and answer questions based on graphs

Third graders explore *probability,* predicting possible outcomes of games with spinners and dice. You may be thinking, "What's that got to do with third grade?" Well, your child has already observed that some events are predictable. We all need to be able to predict certain outcomes or our chances of being successful. When your child plays a game that uses a spinner or dice, probability is involved. Your child will learn basic concepts of *probability,* such as
- recognizing that some events are predictable
- determining if events are certain or impossible

Key Math Skills for Grade 3
Graphing and Probability

- Graphing: selecting appropriate methods to represent data
- Graphing: reading and interpreting pictographs, bar graphs, and line graphs
- Graphing: understanding that one sample's results may not apply to another sample
- Probability: understanding events as certain or impossible, most likely or least likely
- Probability: interpreting outcomes of games
- Probability: making predictions that are based on data (for example, can tell if an event is most likely or least likely)

Name _____   Reading a graph

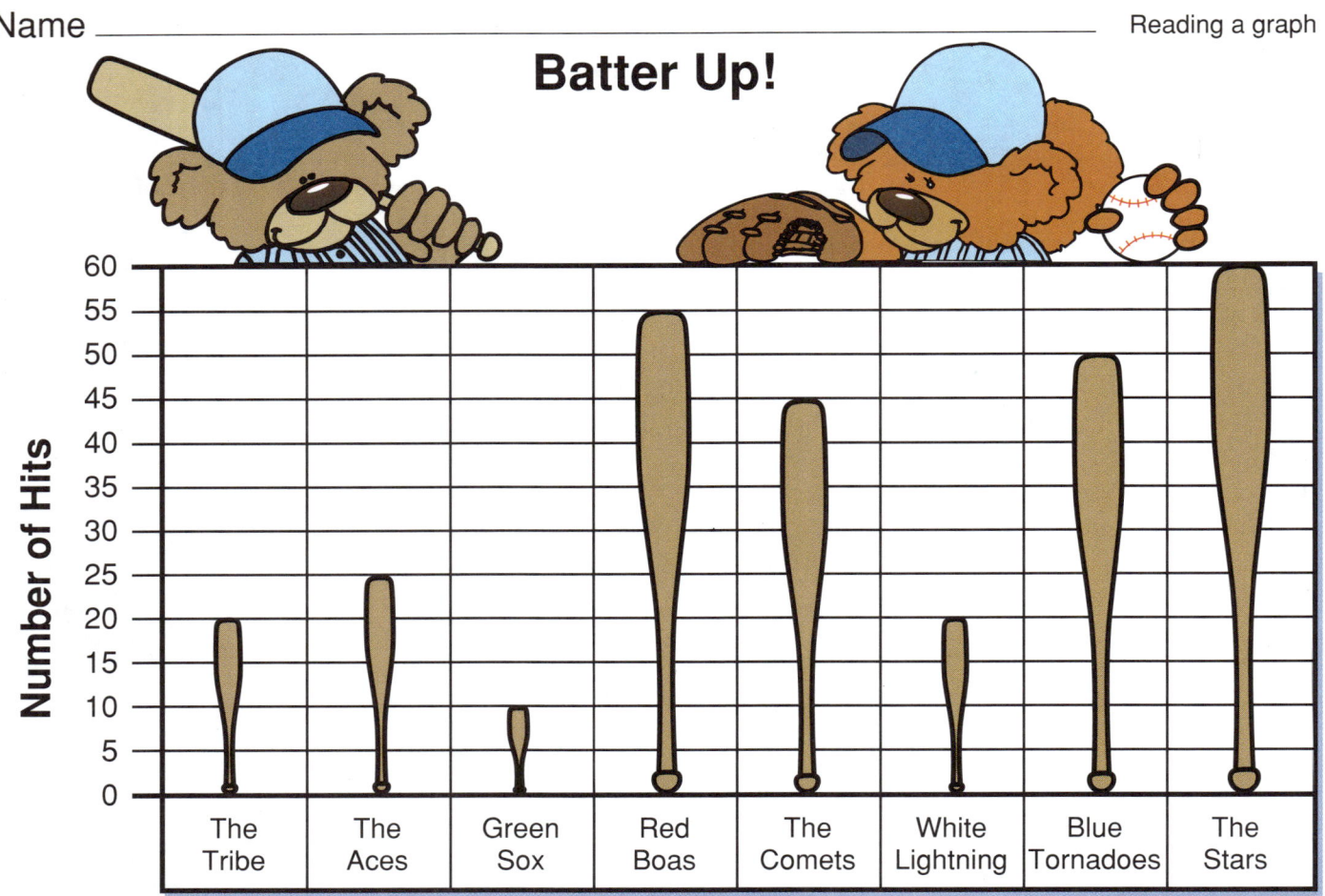

Answer the questions.
Use the graph.

1. Which team made 45 hits? _____

2. Which two teams made more hits than the Blue Tornadoes? _____

3. How many hits did The Aces make? _____

4. Which two teams made the same number of hits? _____

5. Which two teams made more hits than The Comets and fewer hits than The Stars? _____

6. How many more hits did The Stars make than White Lightning? _____

7. Which team had the fewest number of hits? _____

8. How many more hits did the Red Boas make than The Tribe? _____

Name ______________________________

Candy, Candy, Candy!

Graph the number of children who love candies.
Use the information in the box.

CHOCOLATE

mints	10
kisses	11
lollipops	6
gum	5
candy hearts	9
candy bars	12

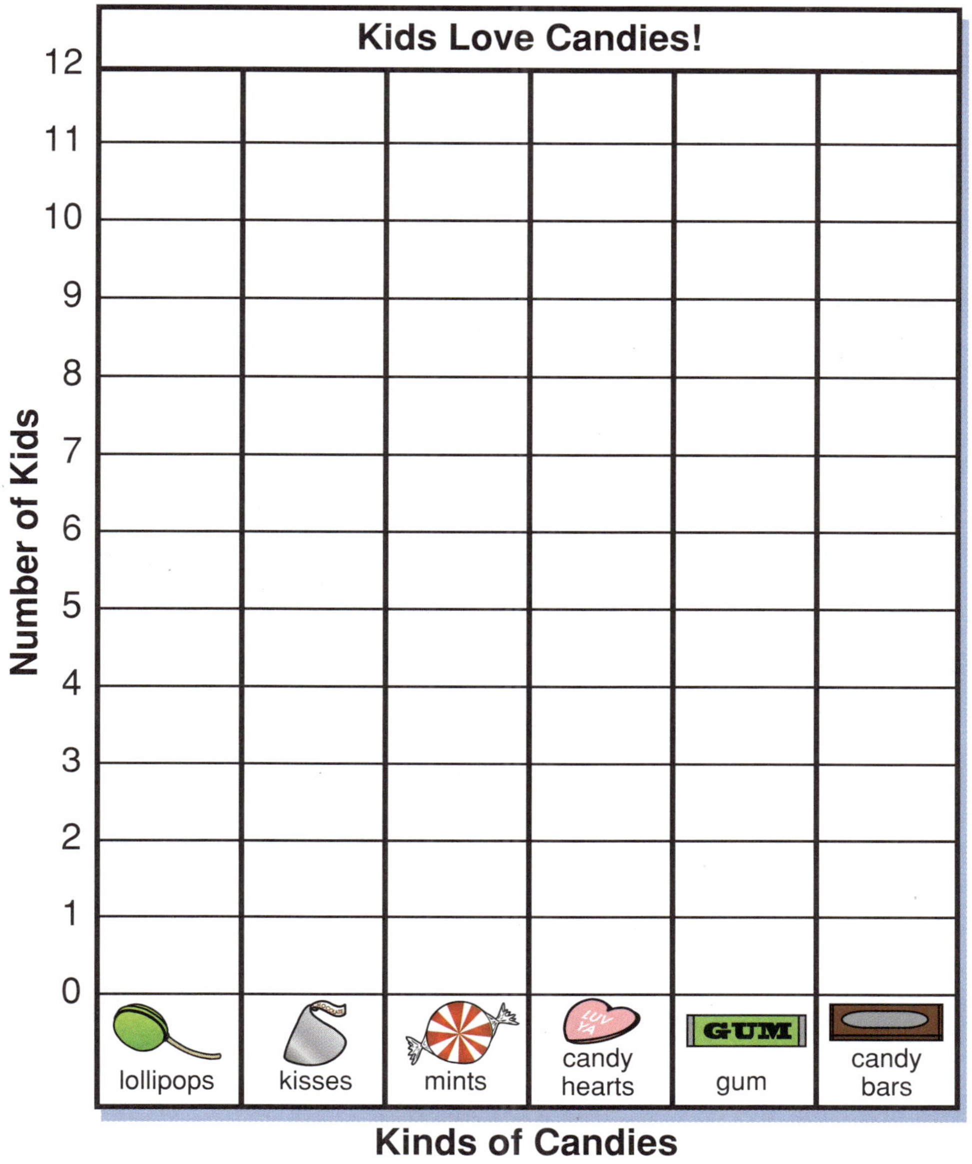
Kids Love Candies!
Number of Kids
12
11
10
9
8
7
6
5
4
3
2
1
0
lollipops
kisses
mints
candy hearts
GUM
gum
candy bars
Kinds of Candies

Use the graph to answer these questions.

1. Which candy is liked by the most children? ______________________
2. Which candy is liked by the fewest children? ______________________
3. How many children like gum? ______________________
4. How many more children like mints than lollipops? ______________________
5. How many more children like kisses than candy hearts? ______________________
6. Which three candies are liked by the most children? ______________________

____

Name_____   Reading a graph

SPEEDY SOLUTIONS!

Sometimes a speedy getaway is the best way for an animal to defend itself against an enemy! Study the graph and read the problems below. Fill in each blank with a word or phrase from the Word Bank that completes the problem. Use each word or phrase once.

Animal Speeds in Miles per Hour

Animal	Speed (mph)
killer whale	35
cheetah	70
sailfish	68
dragonfly	36
zebra	40
rabbit	35
grizzly bear	30
squirrel	12
impala	50
cat	30

Word Bank

greater   total   twice   increase   decreased
half   more than   in all   equal   both

1. A cheetah's speed is _____ as fast as a killer whale's.
2. If an impala runs 25 miles per hour, it's running _____ as fast as its top speed.
3. If a sailfish swimming at its fastest speed slows to 40 mph, it has _____ its speed by 28 mph.
4. To catch up to a zebra running at top speed, a dragonfly must _____ its speed by four mph.
5. A grizzly bear and a cat traveling their fastest will _____ arrive at their destinations at the same time.
6. A rabbit fleeing a grizzly bear must run _____ 30 mph.
7. A squirrel, a dragonfly, and a zebra have a _____ speed of 88 mph.
8. If a killer whale increases its maximum speed by 33 mph, it will travel at a speed _____ to a sailfish's top speed.
9. An impala that runs for 150 miles at a speed of 50 mph has run three hours _____.
10. If a human being can run about 28 mph, nine of the animals can travel at _____ speeds.

102   ©The Education Center, Inc. • Learning Library® • Math • TEC3719

Name_____   Reading a line graph

Valentine Lines

Cupid's Corner Candy Store sells lots of chocolates each Valentine's Day. Look at the line graph below. It shows the number of chocolates sold on Valentine's Day for the past six years. Use the graph to help you answer the questions below. Write your answers on the lines provided.

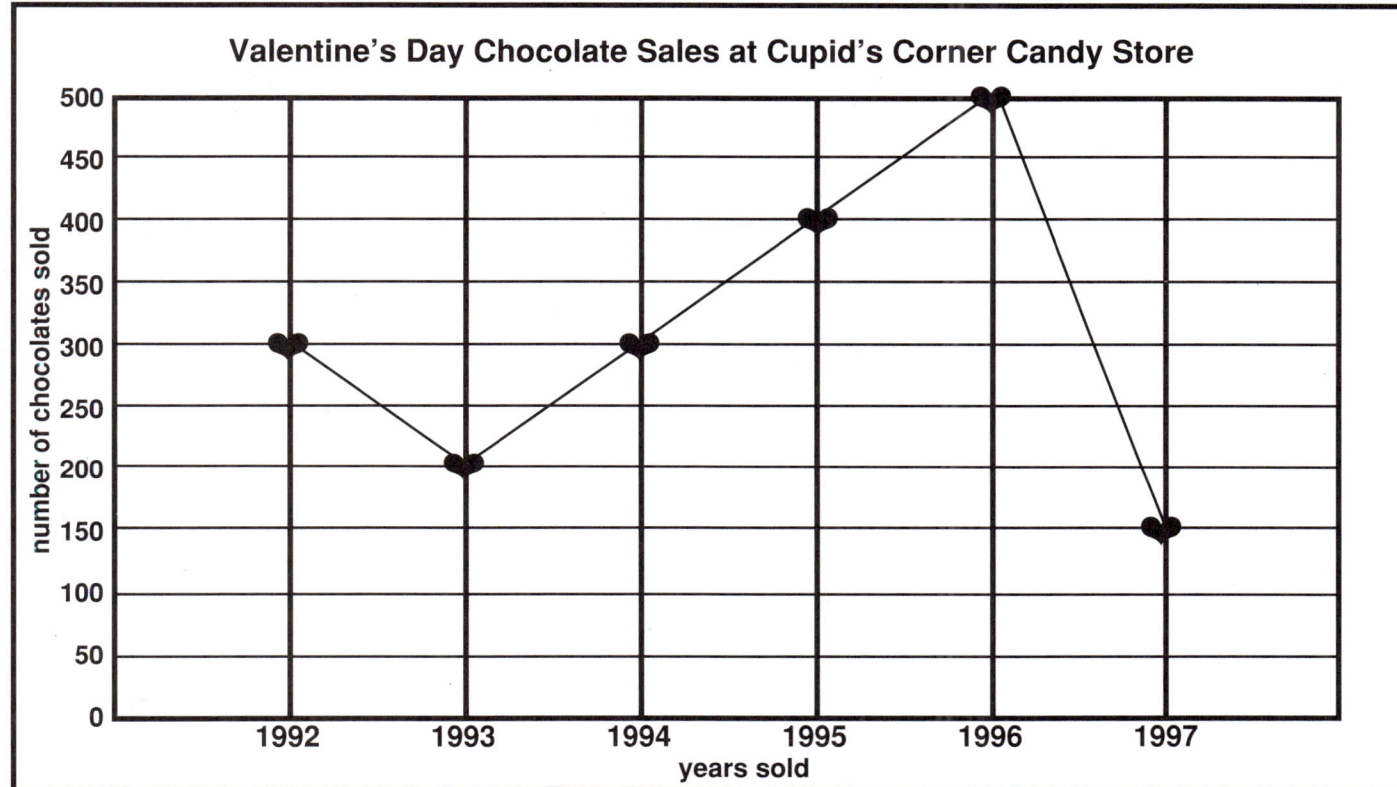

 1. Was the same number of chocolates sold each year? _____

2. During which year were the most chocolates sold? _____

3. During which year were the fewest chocolates sold? _____

4. How many chocolates were sold in 1994? _____

5. Was an equal number of chocolates sold during any years? _____
   If so, which ones? _____

6. During which year were 400 chocolates sold? _____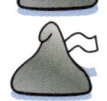

7. How many chocolates were sold in 1996? _____

8. How many chocolates were sold all together in 1992 and 1997? _____

9. How many fewer chocolates were sold in 1993 than in 1996? _____

10. How many more chocolates were sold in 1996 than in 1994? _____

Name_____ Probability: Certain/impossible

Piggy Probability

Write whether picking each item is certain or impossible.

1. A penny from piggy #1 _____

2. A penny from piggy #2 _____

3. A penny from piggy #3 _____

4. A nickel from piggy #1 _____

5. A nickel from piggy #2 _____

6. A nickel from piggy #3 _____

7. A dime from piggy #2 _____

8. A dime from piggy #3 _____

9. A penny or a dime from piggy #1 _____

10. A quarter from piggy #3 _____

Name _____   Probability with a spinner

Dinner Spinner

Just imagine! At this restaurant you can choose the items you'll eat by spinning a spinner!
Write all the possible outcomes for each spinner.
Then write the chance for each outcome.
The first one is done for you.

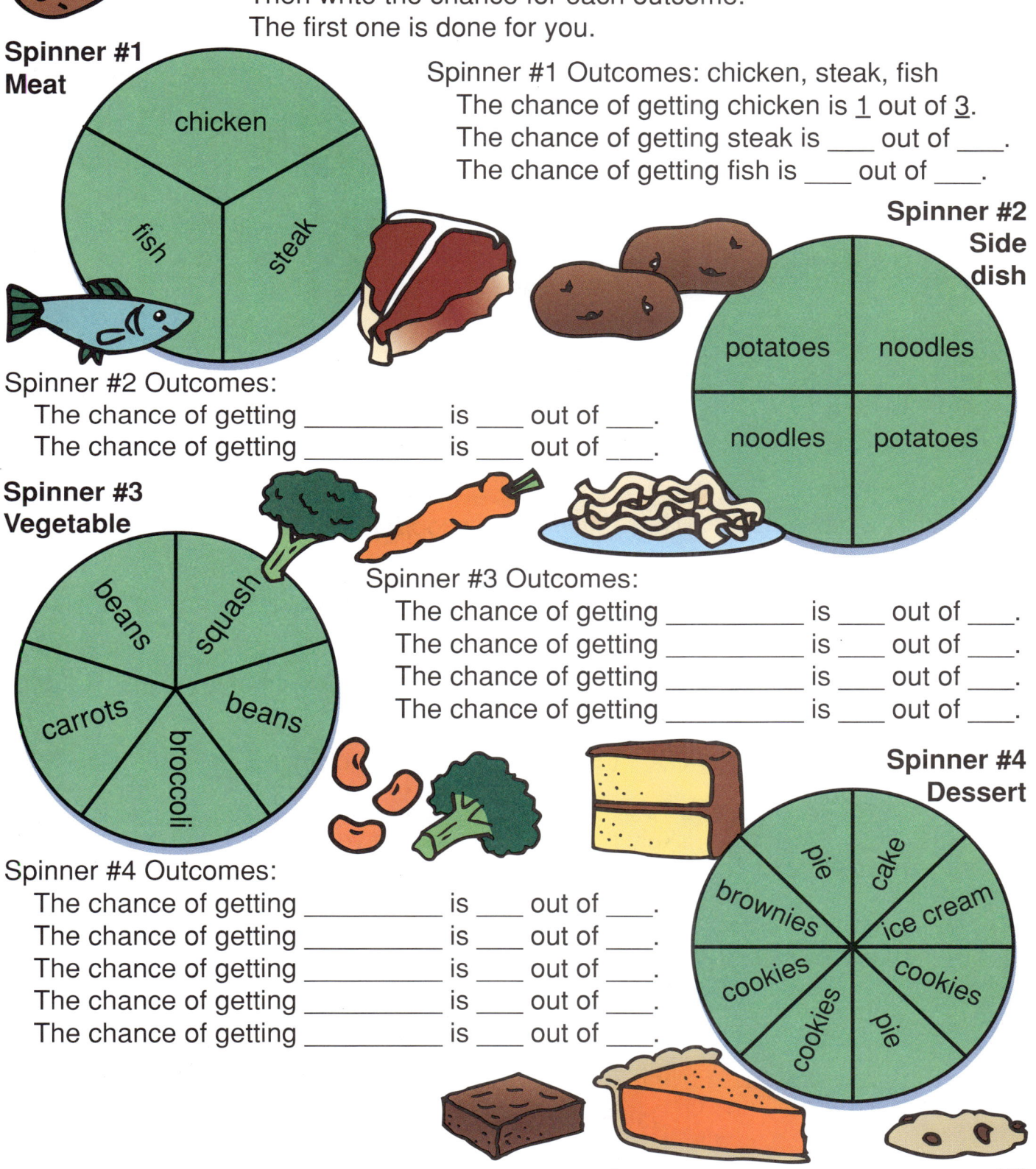

**Spinner #1
Meat**

Spinner #1 Outcomes: chicken, steak, fish
The chance of getting chicken is <u>1</u> out of <u>3</u>.
The chance of getting steak is ___ out of ___.
The chance of getting fish is ___ out of ___.

**Spinner #2
Side dish**

Spinner #2 Outcomes:
The chance of getting _____ is ___ out of ___.
The chance of getting _____ is ___ out of ___.

**Spinner #3
Vegetable**

Spinner #3 Outcomes:
The chance of getting _____ is ___ out of ___.
The chance of getting _____ is ___ out of ___.
The chance of getting _____ is ___ out of ___.
The chance of getting _____ is ___ out of ___.

**Spinner #4
Dessert**

Spinner #4 Outcomes:
The chance of getting _____ is ___ out of ___.
The chance of getting _____ is ___ out of ___.
The chance of getting _____ is ___ out of ___.
The chance of getting _____ is ___ out of ___.
The chance of getting _____ is ___ out of ___.

©The Education Center, Inc. • Learning Library® • Math • TEC3719   105

Name _____   Probability: Least/most likely

Pet Shop Probability

Welcome to Petra's Pet Shop! You may scoop one fish at a time with your net. Write whether each pair of fishy events is *more* likely, *less* likely, or *equally* likely.

Fish Tank A
25 orange fish
5 blue fish

Fish Tank B
5 orange fish
5 yellow fish
5 blue fish

Fish Tank C
10 yellow fish
5 orange fish

1. It is _____ likely that you will scoop an orange fish from Tank A than Tank B.

2. It is _____ likely that you will scoop an orange fish from Tank B than Tank C.

3. It is _____ likely that you will scoop a blue fish than an orange fish from Tank B.

4. It is _____ likely that you will scoop a blue fish than an orange fish from Tank A.

5. It is _____ likely that you will scoop a yellow fish from Tank C than from Tank B.

6. It is _____ likely that you will scoop an orange fish than a blue fish from Tank A.

7. It is _____ likely that you will scoop a yellow fish than an orange fish from Tank C.

8. It is _____ likely that you will scoop a blue fish from Tank B than Tank A.

9. It is _____ likely that you will scoop a blue fish from Tank C than Tank A.

10. It is _____ likely that you will scoop a blue fish from Tank A than an orange fish from Tank C.

Third-Grade Parent Page
Problem Solving

Problem solving pops up in every math unit in third grade, as well as in other content areas. Your child will learn a variety of solving strategies. He will also begin to adapt strategies to reflect his own strengths and learning style.

The strategies your child will explore are working backward, reasoning logically, making a table, finding a pattern, making a list, guessing and checking, and drawing a picture or diagram. He'll learn *key words* that will let him know which strategy is best suited for each type of problem. He will be asked to model these strategies to solve problems.

As your child discovers different ways of reasoning to reach solutions, he'll develop his favorite, most efficient methods to come up with answers. He'll be able to estimate answers, explain his thinking, and discover that solving one kind of problem is related to solving another kind. For instance, subtraction is the inverse operation of addition.

Your child will be challenged to reflect on and discuss his problem-solving methods. You can make the most of real-life problem-solving opportunities by learning the strategies by name and by helping your child apply them appropriately.

Key Math Skills for Grade 3
Problem Solving

- Working backward
- Logical reasoning
- Drawing a picture or Venn diagram
- Making a chart or table
- Making a list
- Guessing and checking
- Estimating
- Finding a pattern
- Acting out the problem

Name _____ Problem solving: Working backward

The Backward Boys

The Backward Boys are the latest singing sensation! They love to do everything backward. Working backward is a strategy that can help you solve problems in math, too. Solve each problem and write its solution in the space provided.

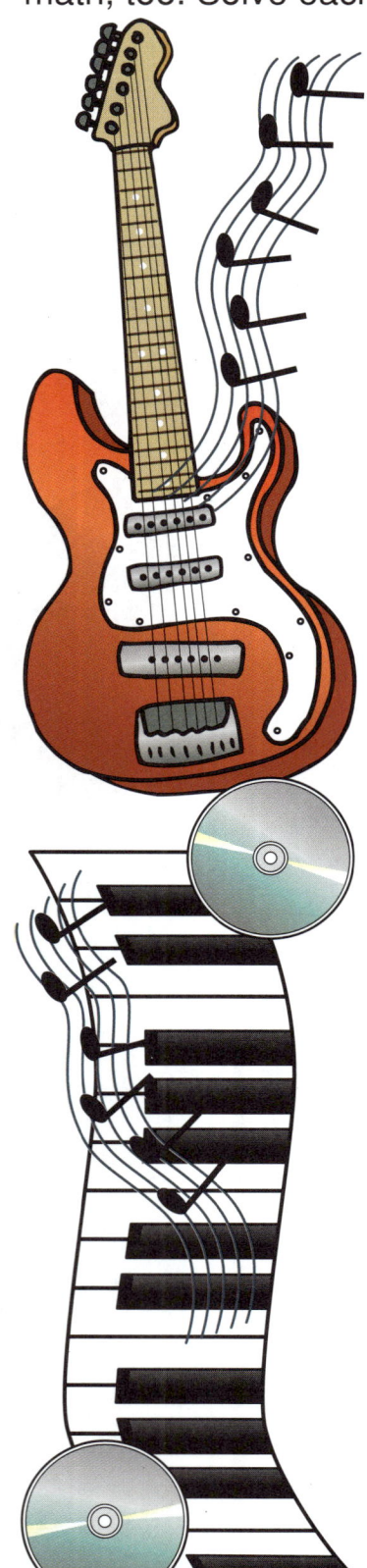

1. Belinda got $4.00 change at the Backward Boys concert. She bought a T-shirt for $16.00, a keyring for $2.00, and a pin for $3.00. How much money did she give the clerk?

   _____

2. The temperature at the outdoor Backward Boys concert was 4 degrees lower at 7:00 than at 6:00. It was 5 degrees lower than that at 8:00. At 8:00 it was 83°F. What was the temperature at 6:00?

   _____

3. The Backward Boys take a water break every 15 minutes during a recording session. When they stopped for the 8th time, it was 6:00. What time did they start recording?

   _____

4. Brodie was given a Backward Boys trading card collection. After 1 month he had 16 more cards. After another month he had 20 more, for a total of 65. How many cards were in the collection Brodie first received?

   _____

5. Brittany's Backward Boys fan club meeting doubled each week. If there were 80 fans at the fourth meeting, how many attended the first one?

   _____

6. Becky bought 3 copies of the latest Backward Boys CDs: one for herself and one each for her two best friends. If each CD cost $8.00 and she got $1.00 change, how much money did she give the clerk?

   _____

Name _____

Problem solving: Logical reasoning

Mail Mix-Up

Sammy Skunk needs your help! He has two postcards to deliver to each house.
Read the delivery clues.
Write the letter of each postcard below the house where it belongs.

Delivery Clues

The house number for the letter marked:

A has digits that total 10.
B is 5 less than 40.
C is less than 36.
D is greater than 35 and less than 39.
E has digits with a difference of 0.

F is 6 more than 25.
G is an odd number.
H is halfway between 30 and 40.
I has matching digits.
J is one less than 40.

Name_____   Problem solving: Drawing a picture (Venn diagram)

After School Is Cool!

"After-School Adventures" is the place to be after 3! Use and construct Venn diagrams to help the adventurers organize the information they have collected about their program.

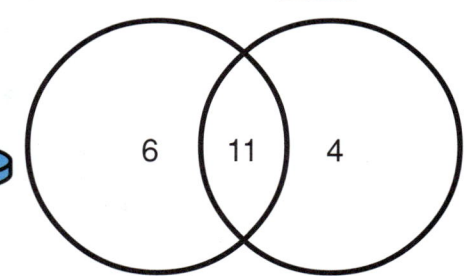

Use this Venn diagram to help you answer the following questions:

1. How many children played board games?
2. How many children participate in both activities?
3. How many children participate in only one activity?

Puzzles   **Board Games**

Complete this Venn diagram using the information below. Then use the diagram to answer the questions.

Garden   **Basketball**

2 work in the garden. 3 play basketball. 6 do both.

4. How many children play basketball?
5. How many children do not work in the garden?

Use the information on the snack chart to complete this Venn diagram. Use it to answer the questions.

Peanut butter—7
Peanut butter & jelly—6
Jelly—8
Banana—5
Jelly & banana—0
Peanut butter & banana—2
Peanut butter & jelly & banana—4

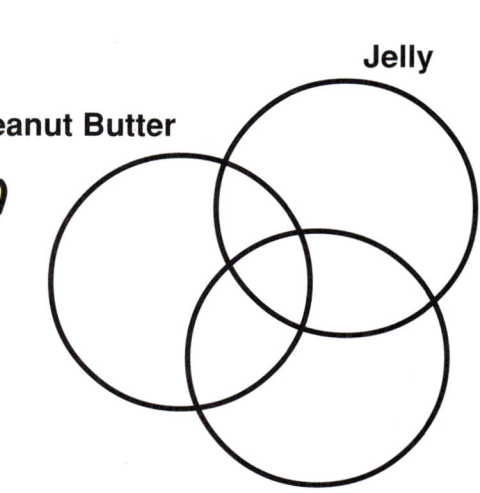

6. How many children ate sandwiches?
7. How many children did not have banana on their sandwiches?
8. How many children had peanut butter on their sandwiches?
9. How many more children had peanut butter & jelly than had peanut butter & banana?
10. Which sandwich is most popular?

Name _____   Problem solving: make a table

Puzzled Over Pancakes

First there was water, then fire, and then cultivated grains. It didn't take long before people started putting it all together, and we've been flipping over flapjacks ever since!

Five children are crazy over these delicious cakes. However, each child enjoys a different topping on his/her flapjacks. Your job is to match each child with the correct favorite topping. Here are the children and the flavors (not in order):

Colby	Chocolate-hazelnut spread
Lacie	Maple syrup
Judson	Strawberries and bananas
Kari	Honey and walnuts
Dev	Apple butter

Use the box below to help you. Put an X in each box that doesn't work and a √ in each box that does. Remember to X out all possibilities that can be eliminated. For example, if you found out that Judson's favorite flavor is maple syrup, you could X out all other flavors for Judson. You could also X out the possibility of another child enjoying the same flavor as Judson.

	Colby	Lacie	Judson	Kari	Dev
Chocolate-hazelnut spread					
Maple syrup					
Strawberries and bananas					
Honey and walnuts					
Apple butter					

Clues:
1. Lacie is allergic to chocolate and she doesn't like apples.
2. Judson thinks syrup and honey are too sticky and thick.
3. Dev's family is the only one that has a banana tree in the backyard.
4. Kari doesn't eat hazelnuts or maple syrup.
5. Colby and Dev are the only children who like honey and walnuts.

Favorite Flapjack Toppings

1. Colby's favorite topping: _____
2. Lacie's favorite topping: _____
3. Judson's favorite topping: _____
4. Kari's favorite topping: _____
5. Dev's favorite topping: _____

Name_____   Problem solving: Find a pattern

Work-It-Out Workout

Help the health nuts at Jim's Gym solve these weighty problems. Look for patterns in the problems. Use the patterns to solve each one, and write the answer in the space provided.

1. Janice could lift 25 pounds the first week she started, 50 pounds the second, and 75 pounds the third. If she continues at the same pace, how many pounds will she be able to lift at 6 weeks?

   _____

2. Julie, the aerobics instructor, had 3 students in her 6:00 class, 6 in her 7:00 class, and 9 in her 8:00 class. If the pattern continues, how many people will be in her 10:00 class?

   _____

3. Jack's weight dropped from 210 pounds to 205 pounds in May. He weighed 200 pounds in June and 195 pounds in July. If he keeps losing weight at the same rate, how much will he weigh in October?

   _____

4. Joan jogged .75 mile on the treadmill on Monday, 1 mile on Tuesday, and 1.25 miles on Wednesday. If the pattern continues, how many miles will she jog on the following Monday?

   _____

5. Jordan's resting heart rate was 81 beats per minute on Monday, 79 beats per minute on Tuesday, 82 on Wednesday, and 78 on Thursday. If the pattern continues, what will Jordan's resting heart rate be on Saturday?

   _____

6. Jennifer loves to snack on health food! She ate 1 oat bran mini-muffin on Monday, 2 on Tuesday, and 3 on Wednesday. If she continues the pattern, how many muffins will she eat in a week?

   _____

Problem solving: Make a list

The Shoppers at the Mall

There is often a lot of information to juggle when solving a problem. Making a list is a strategy that can help you organize information. Then you can manage and understand it better. Use this strategy to solve the problems below. **Hint: Abbreviate words or use a separate sheet of paper.**

The Shopper family is off to the mall! There are many combinations at each shop. Make a list of the possible combinations at each one.

1. Shamir Shopper is looking for shoes. The Shoe Shop carries sneakers, sandals, socks, and ski boots. If Shamir decides to buy 2 of these, list all the possible combinations he can buy.

3. The Shark Shop is the place for Shawn Shopper! He can choose from hammerhead, nurse, and tiger sharks. The shop also carries baby and adult sharks. Finally, Shawn may choose from sharks with or without teeth. List all the possible sharks Shawn may buy.

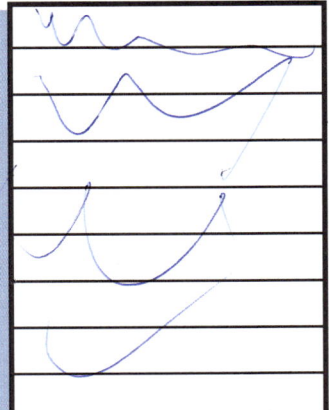

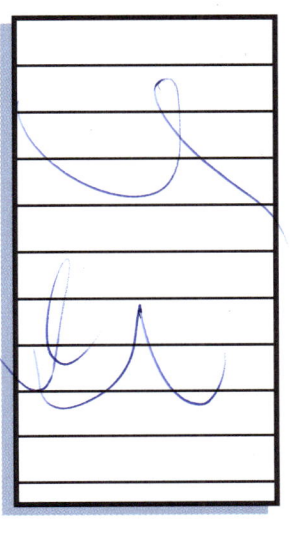

2. Sheldon Shopper loves the Ship Shop. Today's sale is on model ships with 1, 2, or 3 masts. Color choices are blue, red, or yellow. List the possible combinations Sheldon may buy.

4. Sherry Shopper is at the Shell Shop. The shop has brown shells and white shells. There are small, medium, and large shells. List the possible combinations that Sherry may buy.

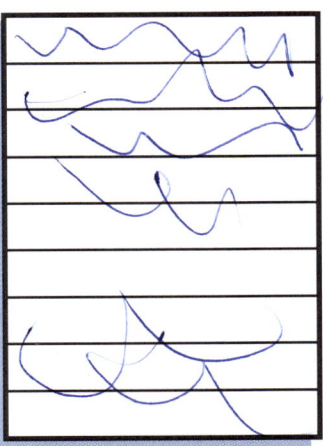

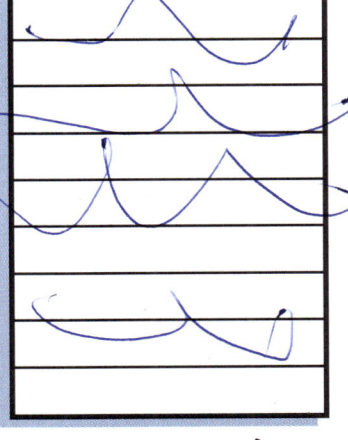

5. Shawna Shopper wants to buy a milk shake, at the Shake Shop, of course! She may choose between strawberry or shortcake ice cream, thick or thin milk shake, one straw or two, and regular or jumbo. List all the possible combinations she may buy.

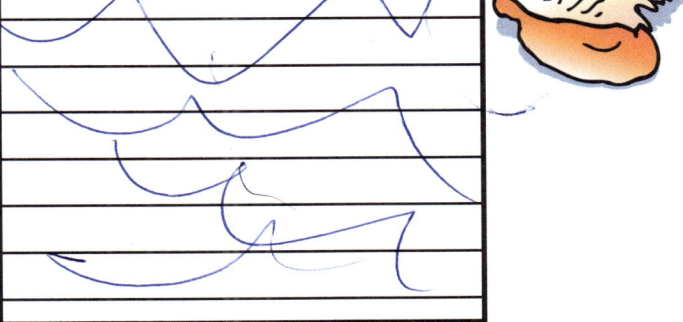

Name_____   Problem solving: Guess and check

In My Pockets
Sometimes you can solve a problem like this:
- Read the problem.
- Guess a reasonable answer.
- Check your answer.
- Adjust your answer.
- Guess again!
- Keep guessing until your answer works.

Try this "guess and check" strategy to solve these problems. Show your work and write your answers in the spaces provided.

1. There are 3 more marbles than shells in this pocket. There are 13 marbles and shells in all. How many shells are there? How many marbles are there?

2. I have 7 coins in this pocket for a total of $1.25. What coins do I have?

3. I have twice as many mints as fruit chews in this pocket. I have 21 pieces of candy all together. How many mints do I have?

4. In my two pockets there are a total of 24 peanuts. One pocket has 2 more peanuts than the other. How many peanuts are in each pocket?

5. There are 20 feathers and acorns in this pocket. I have $1/3$ as many acorns as feathers. How many acorns do I have? How many feathers?

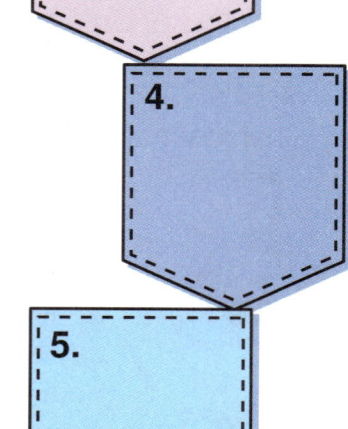

114   ©The Education Center, Inc. • Learning Library® • Math • TEC3719

Name _____   Problem solving: Multiplication/division

Garden Grocer

It's time to take your harvest to market! Use the price list to solve the problems. Show your work.

SALE!
Radishes—40¢ per bunch
Carrots—7¢ each
Squash—10¢ each
Beans—3¢ each
Corn—8¢ per ear
Strawberries—4¢ each

1. How much will 3 carrots cost?
   _____

2. How much will twice as many carrots cost?
   _____

3. If there are 8 radishes in a bunch, how much does each radish cost?
   _____

4. How much will 7 ears of corn cost?
   _____

5. How much will half a dozen strawberries cost?
   _____

6. If a customer spends 60¢ on squash, how many did he buy?
   _____

7. How many nickels does a customer need to buy a bunch of radishes?
   _____

8. If a customer has 35¢ to spend, how many carrots can she buy?
   _____

9. You decide to package your strawberries in baskets that will cost 20¢. How many strawberries will be in each basket?
   _____

10. How much will 8 beans cost?
    _____

At Home: Create and solve problems like these. Save the sale circulars from grocery stores or your local newspaper. Have your child cut and paste items to illustrate his problems.

Answer Keys

Page 6

Page 7

Page 8

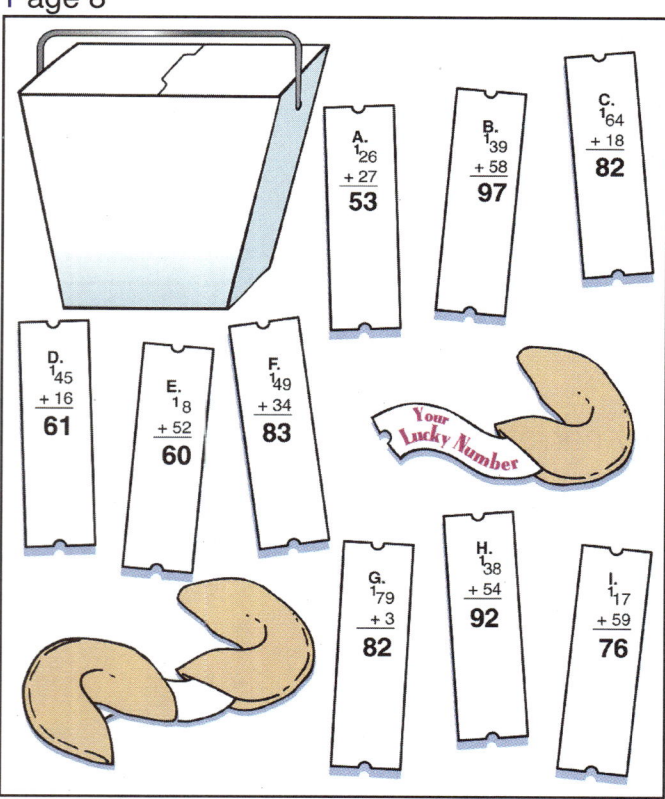

Page 9

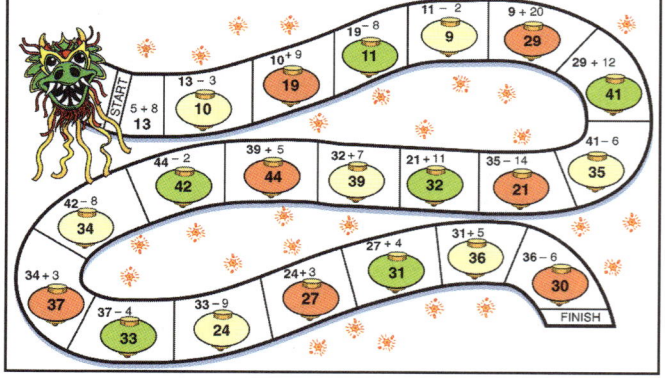

Page 10

Example: $^3\,^12$ $\cancel{4}\cancel{2}$ -19 $\overline{23}$ = S	$^5\,^14$ $\cancel{6}\cancel{4}$ -38 $\overline{26}$ = L	$^6\,^17$ $\cancel{7}\cancel{7}$ -29 $\overline{48}$ = A	$^6\,^15$ $\cancel{7}\cancel{5}$ -46 $\overline{29}$ = R	$^1\,^14$ $\cancel{2}\cancel{4}$ -17 $\overline{7}$ = N
$^7\,^12$ $\cancel{8}\cancel{2}$ -33 $\overline{49}$ = D	$^2\,^12$ $\cancel{3}\cancel{2}$ -16 $\overline{16}$ = K	$^4\,^16$ $\cancel{5}\cancel{6}$ -9 $\overline{47}$ = P	$^3\,^11$ $\cancel{4}\cancel{1}$ -17 $\overline{24}$ = W	$^5\,^11$ $\cancel{6}\cancel{1}$ -24 $\overline{37}$ = G
$^8\,^14$ $\cancel{9}\cancel{4}$ -86 $\overline{8}$ = O	$^7\,^17$ $\cancel{8}\cancel{7}$ -8 $\overline{79}$ = H	$^8\,^13$ $\cancel{9}\cancel{3}$ -39 $\overline{54}$ = I	$^2\,^17$ $\cancel{3}\cancel{7}$ -9 $\overline{28}$ = E	$^6\,^11$ $\cancel{7}\cancel{1}$ -33 $\overline{38}$ = T

G L O W - I N - T H E - D A R K
37 26 8 24   54 7   38 79 28   49 48 29 16

R E P - T I L E S
29 28 47   38 54 26 28 23

Page 11

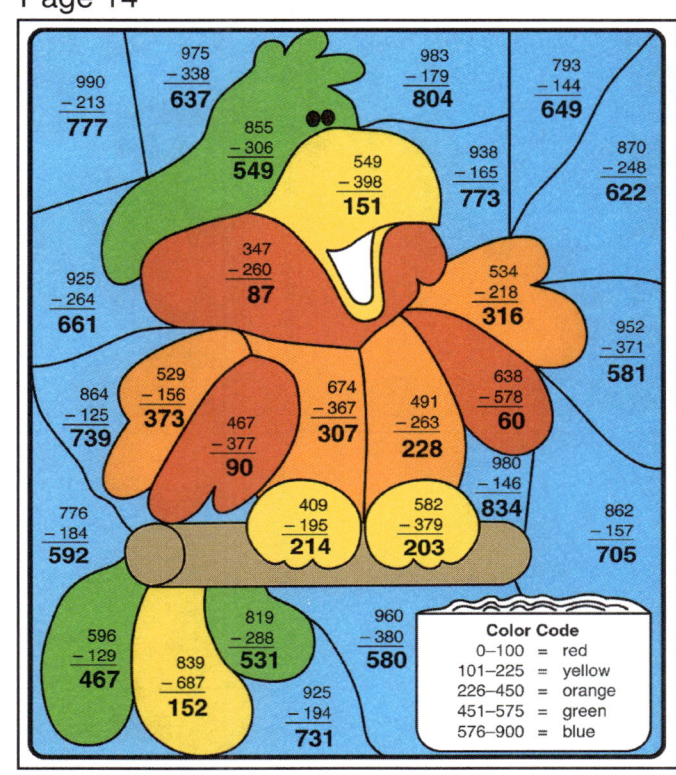

To solve the riddle, match the letters to the numbered lines below.

What do you get when you cross an elephant with a fish?

E N O R M O U S   S W I M M I N G
79 22 70 50 35 55 24 19   99 92 94 43 98 87 27 29

T R U N K S !
23 75 90 44 33 66

Page 12

1. 4
2. 12
3. 14
4. 16
5. 20
6. 19
7. 17
8. 15
9. 9
10. 7

Page 14

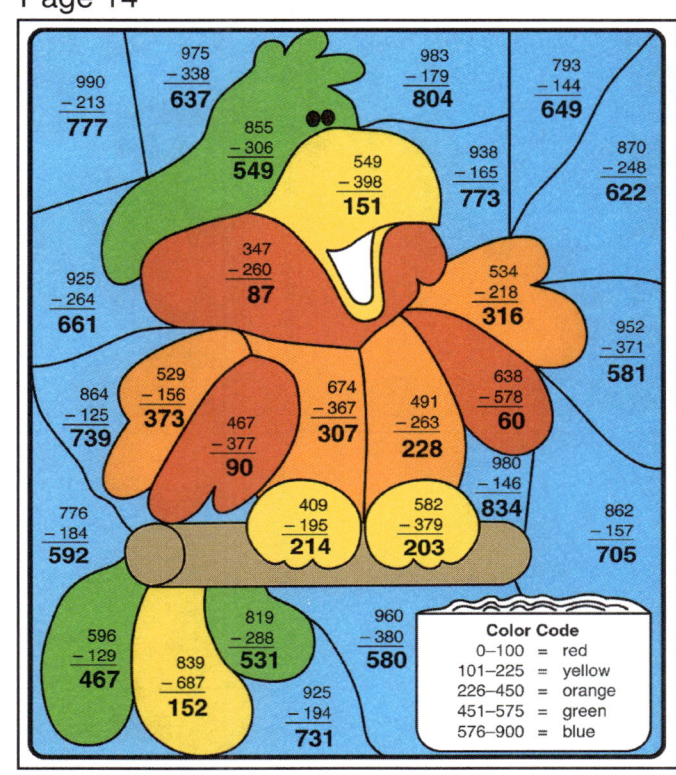

Page 13

1. 73 cows
2. 49 biscuits
3. 70 horses
4. 18 tickets
5. 16 bales
6. 31 animals
7. 5 ponies
8. 6 coyotes
9. 51 jackrabbits
10. 42 riders

Page 15

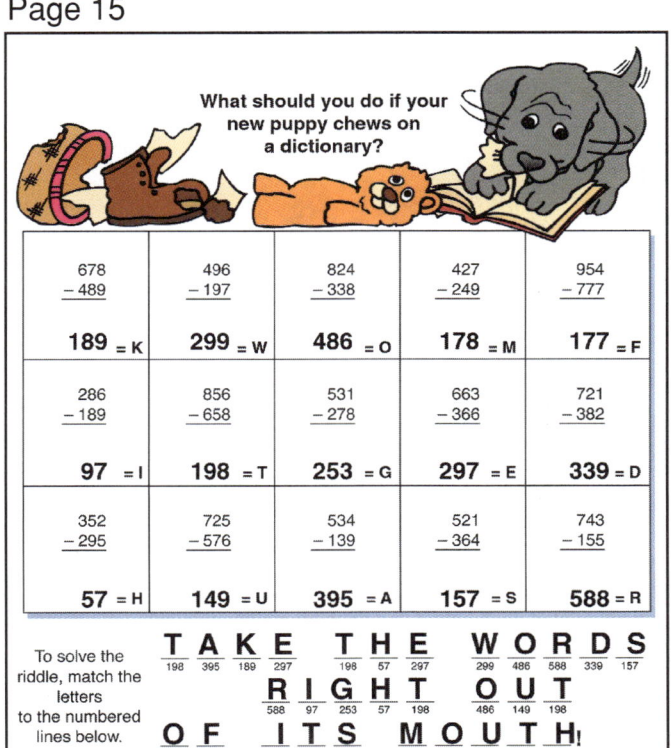

To solve the riddle, match the letters to the numbered lines below.

T A K E   T H E   W O R D S
198 395 189 297   198 57 297   299 486 588 339 157

R I G H T   O U T
588 97 253 57 198   486 149 198

O F   I T S   M O U T H !
486 177   97 198 157   178 486 149 198 57

Page 16

Page 17

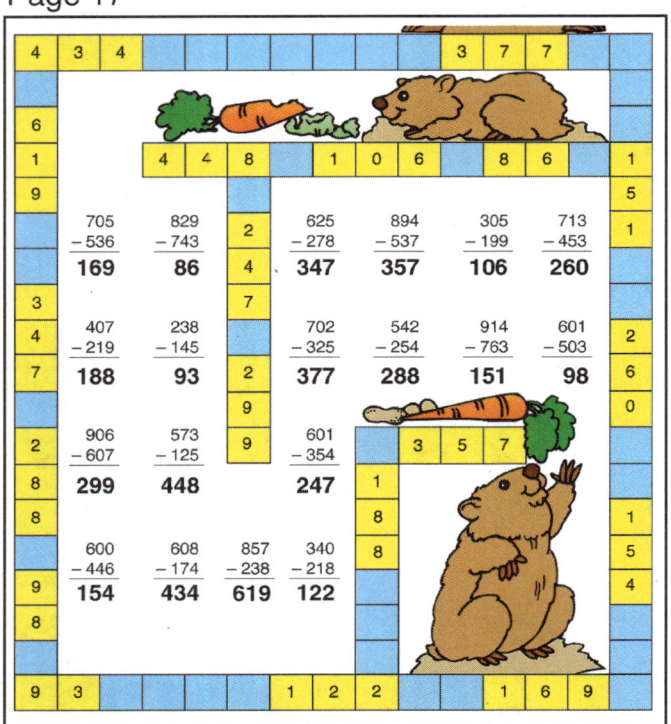

Page 18

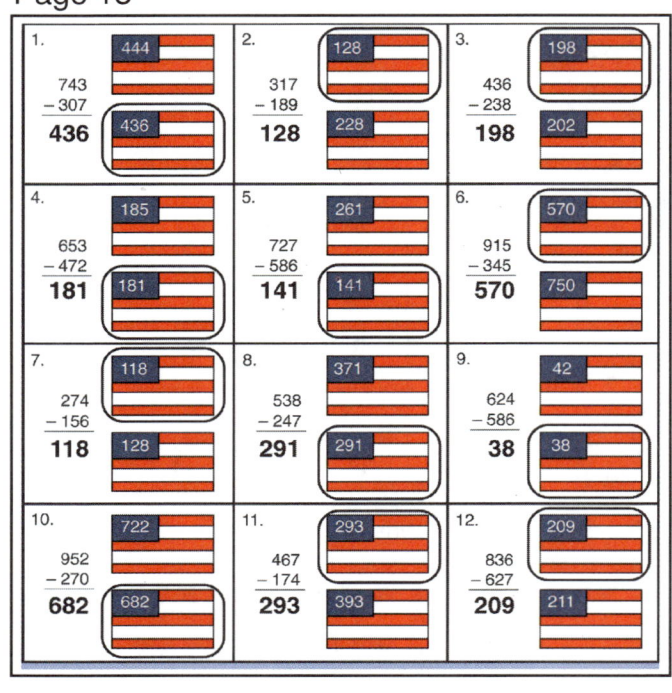

Page 22
A. 156, 516, 615, 651
B. 213, 437, 440, 537
C. 166, 606, 616, 669
D. 109, 111, 201, 209
E. 28, 80, 82, 280
F. 818, 888, 953, 980

Page 23

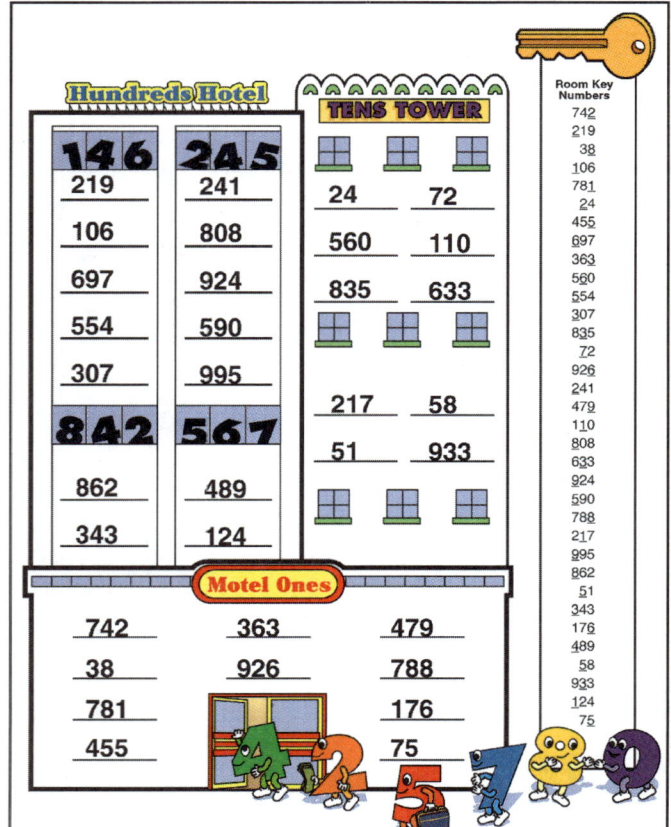

Page 24

Page 25
A. 2,539
B. 4,106
C. 1,972
D. 5,285
E. 9,458
F. 3,721
G. 7,863
H. 8,640
I. 6,314
J. 3,197
K. 5,005
L. 1,273
M. 9,632
N. 4,958

Page 26

Page 27

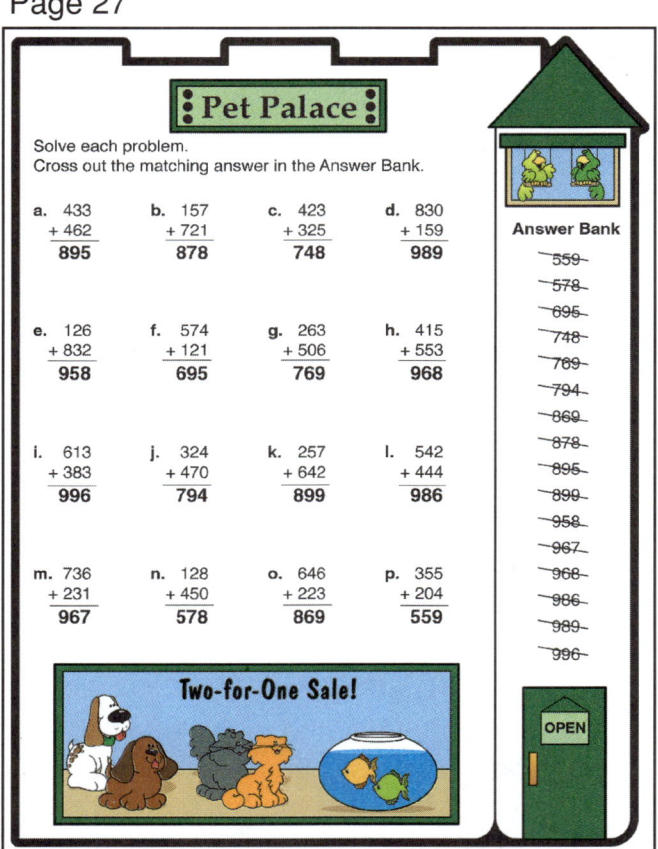

Page 28

Page 29
1. 56 + 124 = 180
2. 124 + 92 = 216
3. 92 + 79 = 171
4. 59 + 201 = 260
5. 201 + 189 = 390
6. 189 + 43 = 232

Page 30

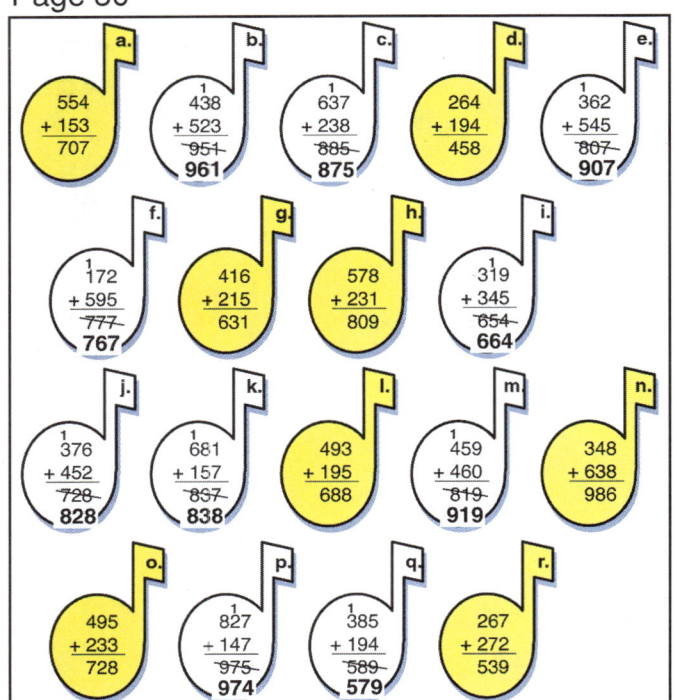

Page 31

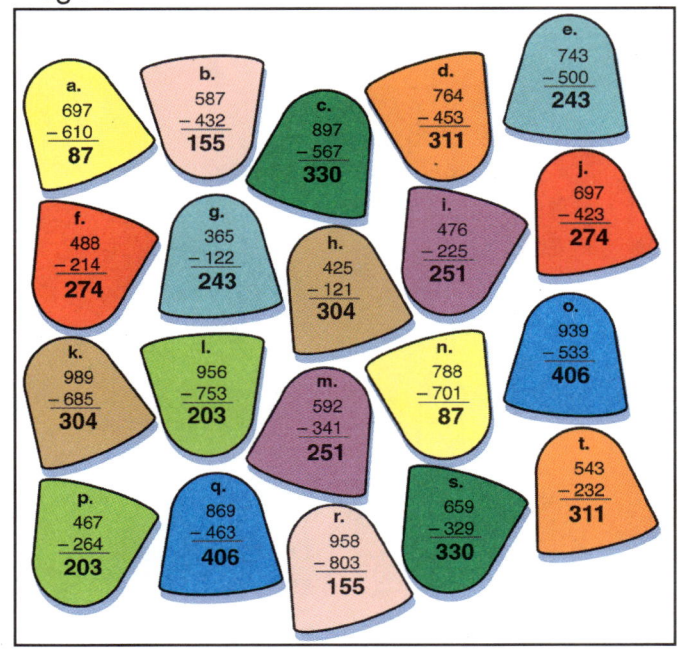

Page 32

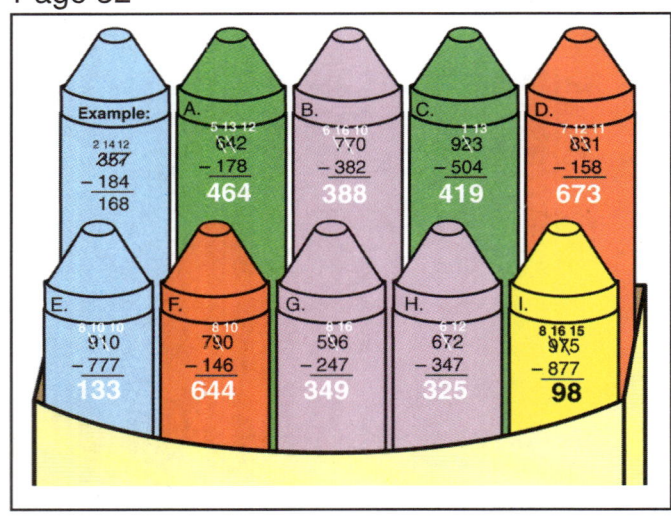

Page 33
A. 327
B. 462
C. 544
D. 252
E. 237
F. 60
G. 644
H. 91
I. 177
J. 644
K. 192

Page 37
Write the equation and multiply to find how many carrots Fred needs to make.
1. 5 bunches of 6   5 x 6 = 30
2. 6 bunches of 5   6 x 5 = 30
3. 8 bunches of 4   8 x 4 = 32
4. 8 bunches of 6   8 x 6 = 48
5. 9 bunches of 4   9 x 4 = 36
6. 4 bunches of 6   4 x 6 = 24
7. 7 bunches of 5   7 x 5 = 35
8. 8 bunches of 5   8 x 5 = 40
9. 7 bunches of 8   7 x 8 = 56
10. 1 jumbo bunch of 32   1 x 32 = 32

Page 34

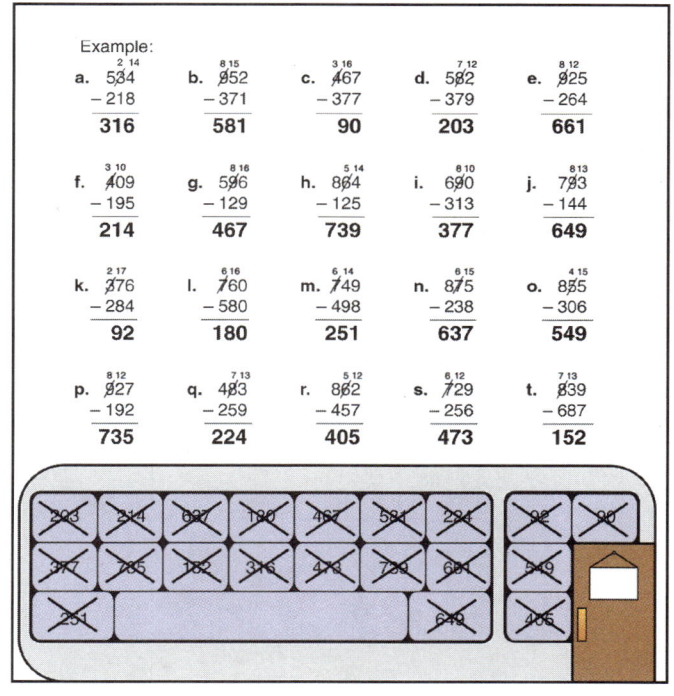

Page 35

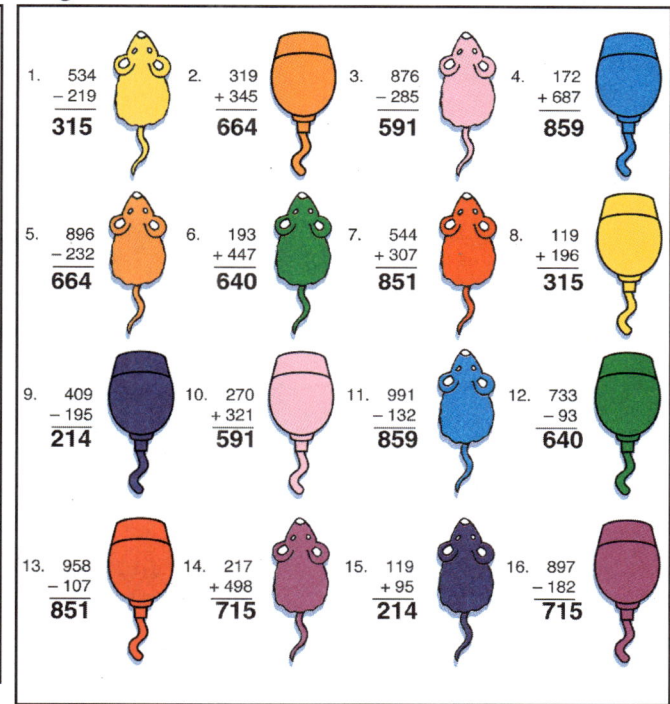

Page 38

Page 39
Answers will vary.

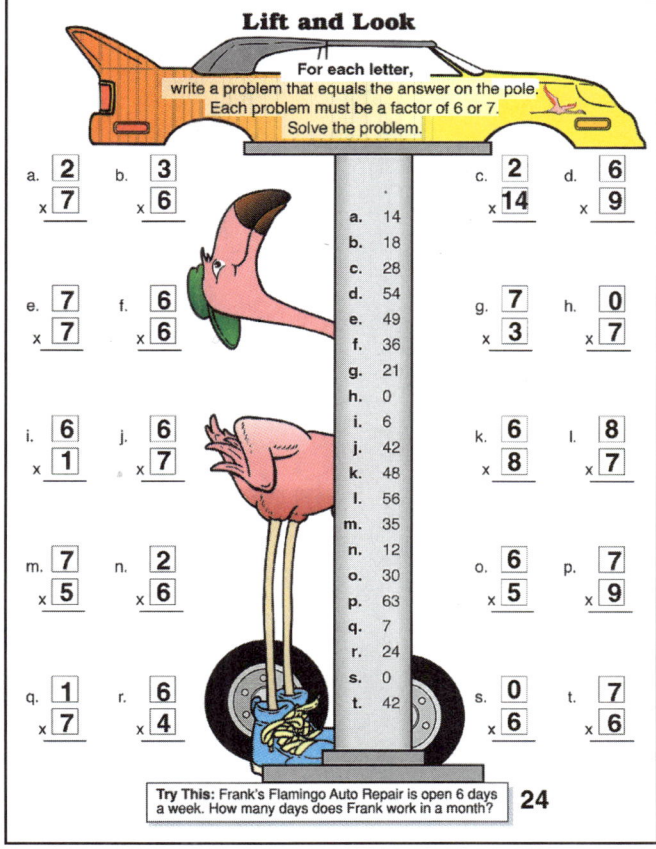

Page 40

a. △ x 7 = **49**   9 x ⑨ = **81**   ⑨ x 4 = **36**

b. 2   △   3   ⑧   6   ⑨   ⑧
   x⑧   x 8   x⑨   x 9   x△   x 8   x 5
   16 **56** **27** **72** **42** **72** **40**

c. 2 x ⑨ = **18**   7 x ⑧ = **56**   ⑧ x 4 = **32**

d. △   5   ⑨   ⑧   △   ⑧   5
   x 4   x△   x 7   x 1   x 2   x 8   x⑨
   28 **35** **63**   **8** **14** **64** **45**

e. ⑨ x 6 = **54**   7 x △ = **49**   9 x ⑧ = **72**

f. 1   ⑧   5   3   ⑨   5   △
   x△   x 6   x⑨   x△   x 1   x⑧   x 9
    7 **48** **45** **21**   **9** **40** **63**

Page 41

2 x 7 = 14 ⑧ x6=48 2 x8=16 1 x7=7 5 x8=40 3 x5=15 9 x7=63 3 x8=24 6 x7=42 9 x5=45
5 x 5 = 25   8 x9=72
3 x 9 = 27 9 x8=72 5 x9=45 7 x6=42 4 x9=36 6 x5=30 2 x6=12 6 x8=48
0 x 6 = 0   2 x5=10
7 x 8 = 56 0 x5=0 8 x8=64 1 x6=6 8 x7=56 2 x9=18 5 x7=35 0 x8=0
1 x 5 = 5   9 x9=81
4 x 7 = 28
5 x 6 = 30   1 x8=8
4 x 8 = 32 7 x5=35 7 x7=49 9 x6=54 3 x7=21 0 x9=0 4 x5=20 3 x6=18
0 x 7 = 0
4 x 6 = 24
6 x 9 = 54
1 x 9 = 9
8 x 5 = 40
7 x 9 = 63
6 x 6 = 36

Page 42

1. ⑨ x ③ = **27**   11. ② x ⑨ = **18**
2. ⑥ x ② = **12**   12. ④ x ④ = **16**
3. ⑤ x ⑤ = **25**   13. ③ x ③ = **9**
4. ① x ⑧ = **8**   14. ④ x ⑦ = **28**
5. ⑦ x ⑨ = **63**   15. ⑧ x ⑨ = **72**
6. ⑥ x ⑥ = **36**   16. ⑤ x ① = **5**
7. ① x ⑦ = **7**   17. ④ x ⑧ = **32**
8. ⑨ x ⑨ = **81**   18. ⑦ x ④ = **28**
9. ② x ④ = **8**   19. ③ x ⑥ = **18**
10. ⑧ x ⑤ = **40**   20. ⑧ x ② = **16**

Page 43

A. Best Gas Three gallons — 36¢
B. Cheap Gas Five gallons — 50¢
C. Cheap Gas Eight gallons — 80¢
D. Good Gas Six gallons — 66¢
E. Best Gas Ten gallons — $1.20
F. Cheap Gas Four gallons — 40¢
G. Good Gas Nine gallons — 99¢
H. Cheap Gas Twelve gallons — $1.20
I. Best Gas Seven gallons — 84¢
J. Good Gas Eleven gallons — $1.21
K. Good Gas Two gallons — 22¢
L. Best Gas Five gallons — 60¢

Best Gas = 12¢ per gallon
Good Gas = 11¢ per gallon
Cheap Gas = 10¢ per gallon

Bonus Box: Color each ticket.
Pink = total is more than 75¢
Yellow = total is less than 75¢

Page 44

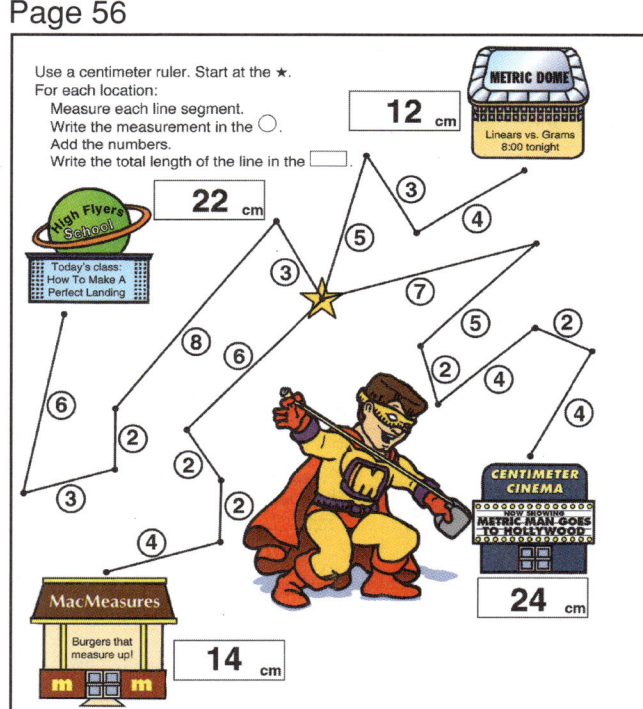

Page 45

8 x5 **40**	6 x8 **48**	2 x2 **4**	9 x8 **72**	3 x7 **21**	4 x1 **4**	5 x3 **15**	7 x8 **56**
8 x2 **16**	4 x4 **16**	6 x4 **24**	2 x3 **6**	7 x2 **14**	9 x4 **36**	3 x6 **18**	7 x1 **7**
5 x5 **25**	6 x0 **0**	3 x8 **24**	7 x7 **49**	4 x0 **0**	6 x6 **36**	7 x9 **63**	4 x2 **8**
6 x2 **12**	8 x4 **32**	5 x7 **35**	4 x7 **28**	6 x5 **30**	4 x9 **36**	3 x4 **12**	5 x8 **40**

Page 47
1. 7 plants
2. 9 seeds
3. 6 potatoes
4. 10 plants
5. 6 bunches
6. 3 rows
7. 1 beetle

Page 53
1. 3/6, 2/6, 1/6
2. 2/4, 1/4, 1/4
3. 1/2, 1/2
4. 1/3, 2/3

Page 57
A. 4 cm (yellow)
B. 17 cm (purple)
C. 12 cm (red)
D. 15 cm (green)
E. 11 cm (yellow)
F. 12 cm (red)
G. 24 cm (purple)
H. 21 cm (purple)
I. 12 cm (red)
J. 14 cm (green)

Page 56

Page 59
A. 54 sq. cm
B. 32 sq. cm
C. 4 sq. cm
D. 9 sq. cm
E. 25 sq. cm
F. 36 sq. cm
G. 34 sq. cm

Page 60
1. −5° C
2. 58° F
3. 65° F
4. 45° F
5. 90° F
6. 18° C
7. 85° F
8. 75° F
9. 37° C
10. 35° F

Page 62
1. pumpkin — 7 lb. (1 lb.) 7 oz.
2. crown — 5 oz. (5 lb.) 50 lb.
3. pumpkin coach — 1 lb. 1 oz. (1 ton)
4. magic beans — 1 lb. (1 oz.) 10 oz.
5. brick — (1 lb.) 1 oz. 10 lb.
6. apple — 3 lb. (8 oz.) 16 oz.
7. straw — 2 lb. (20 lb.) 2 tons
8. book of magic — 2 oz. 2 tons (2 lb.)
9. glass slippers — (3 lb.) 13 lb. 33 lb.
10. throne — 2 lb. 22 lb. (222 lb.)
11. frog — (1 lb.) 1 oz. 1 ton

At Home: Gather several household items. Estimate the weight of each and record your estimate. Then weigh the item and compare the actual weight with your estimate. Keep practicing!

Page 63

Page 64

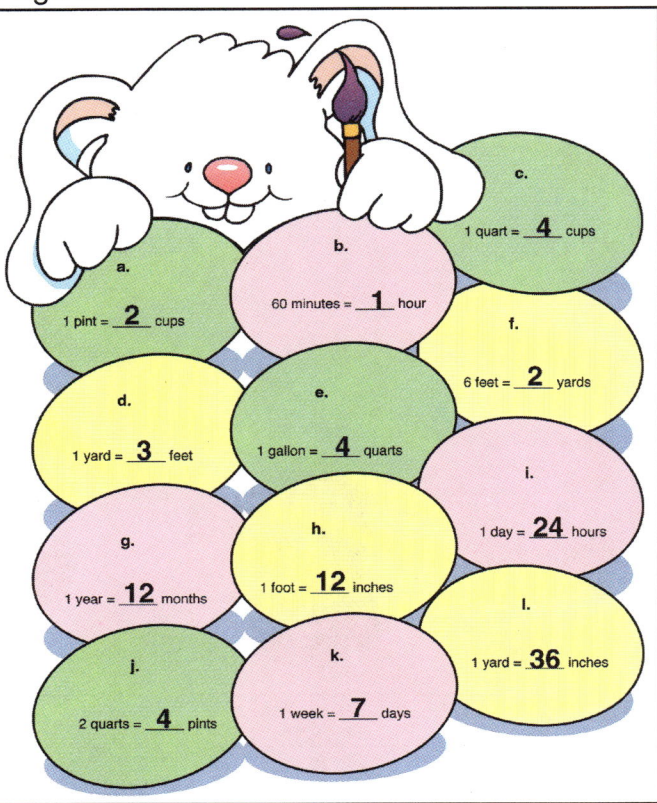

Page 69
1. 4:05
2. 9:15
3. 12:20
4. 9:40
5. 8:00
6. 12:50
7. 5:35
8. 7:45
9. 1:45

Page 70
c, h, k, a, f, i, d, g, e, j, l, b

Page 72
4. early
5. 2 hours and 30 minutes
6. morning
7. dinner
8. 6:10 A.M.
9. 11:20 A.M., eleven twenty A.M.
10. 4:50 P.M., four fifty P.M.

Page 73
1. 9 1/2 hours
2. yes; answers will vary
3. 7:55 A.M.
4. 1 hour 25 minutes
5. 3 hours 45 minutes
6. 8:25 P.M.
7. 35 minutes
8. 3:20 P.M.
9. 55 minutes
10. 6:30 P.M.

Page 74
1. $0.55
2. $0.75
3. $1.10
4. $2.00
5. $5.00
6. $24.25
7. $18.60
8. $22.22
9. $7.99
10. $0.05

Page 75

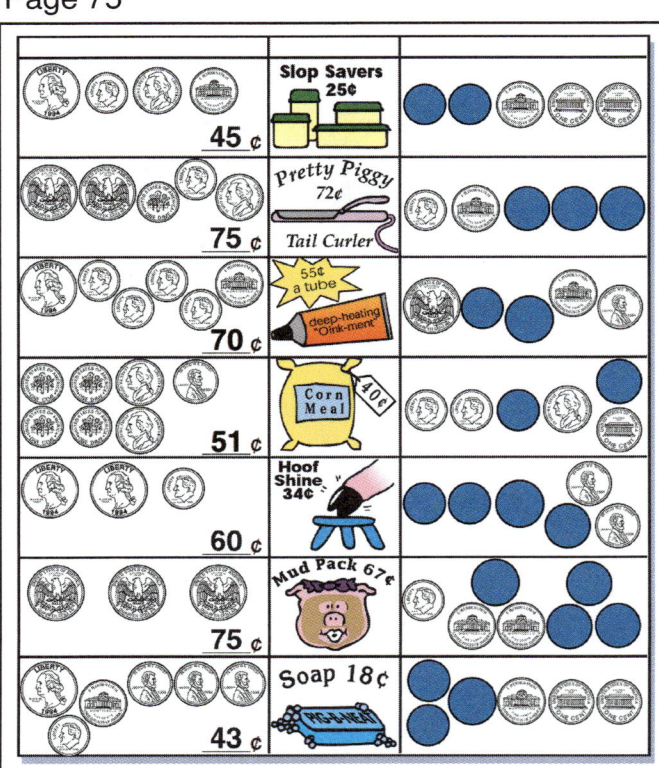

Page 76

Order #1	
club	3.00
jelly	.34
cheese	.31
catsup	.10
Total	$ 3.75

Order #2	
poor boy	2.00
peanut butter	.30
dill pickle	.25
barbecue sauce	.12
Total	$ 2.67

Order #3	
open face	3.00
banana	.32
mustard	.10
hot fudge	.16
Total	$ 3.58

Order #4	
torpedo	2.00
tuna fish	.33
jelly	.34
marshmallow creme	.20
Total	$ 2.87

Order #5	
hoagie	2.00
cheese	.31
barbecue sauce	.12
dill pickle	.25
Total	$ 2.68

Order #6	
pita	3.00
peanut butter	.30
whipped cream	.14
catsup	.10
Total	$ 3.54

Page 77
1. $2.50
2. $0.10
3. $0.16
4. $0.50
5. $3.00
6. $2.90

Page 81
(Each student should have shown one drawing in each box. However, a variety of possible answers is shown below.)

Polygons	How can a polygon of this type be made...	How can a polygon of this type be made...
A. triangles — 3 sides 3 angles	with 2 triangles?	with 4 triangles?
B. quadrilaterals — 4 sides 4 angles	with 2 triangles?	with 4 triangles?
C. pentagons — 5 sides 5 angles	with 3 triangles?	with 4 triangles?
D. hexagons — 6 sides 6 angles	with 4 triangles?	a different way with 4 triangles?

Page 82
1. A, L
2. B, K
3. C, F
4. D, N
5. E, P
6. G, M
7. H, O
8. I, T
9. J, Q
10. R, S

Page 83
1. line segment
2. line
3. line segment
4. ray
5. line segment
6. ray
7. ray
8. line
9. ray
10. line

Page 84
1. right
2. greater
3. right
4. less
5. less
6. greater

Page 90

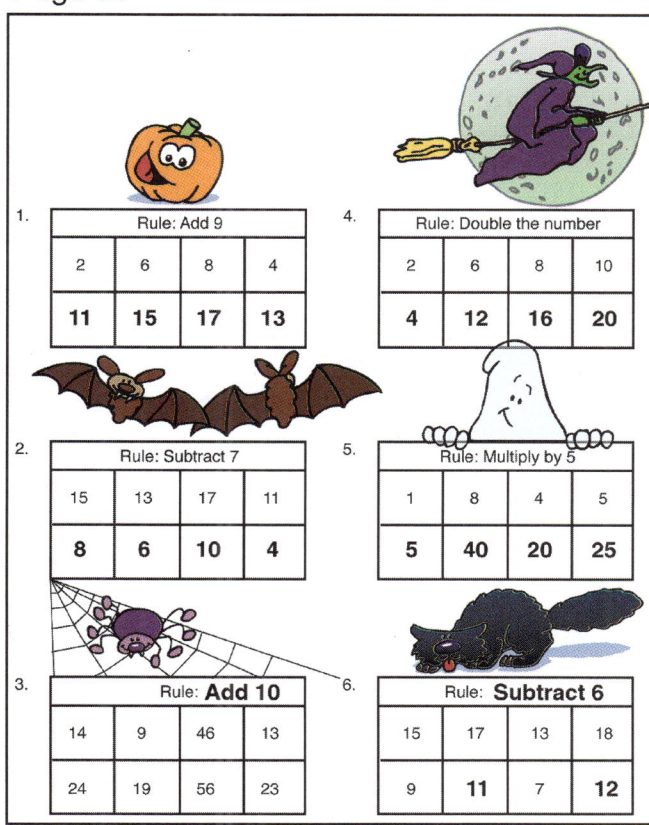

125

Page 91
1. 11 bags
2. 4 pieces
3. 4 hours
4. 4 balls
5. $0.15
6. 7 prizes
7. 4 x 0 = 0
8. 6 x 6 = 36
9. 1 x 7 = 7
10. 9 x 8 = 72
11. 9 x 2 = 18
12. 3 x 3 = 9

Page 93
1. 16
2. 19
3. 30
4. 92
5. 41
6. 60

Try This:
6 x 6 + 6 = 42
9 x 5 + 7 = 52

Page 94

Page 95
1. pence
2. peso
3. franc
4. centavo
5. fils
6. yen
7. lira
8. kobo
1. (10, 8) (5, 10) (1, 11) (7, 1) (10, 4) (6, 7) (7, 1)
2. (11, 1) (8, 3) (11, 9) (6, 7)
3. (12, 6) (8, 3) (4, 1) (8, 9) (6, 7) (5, 5)
4. (2, 5) (6, 7) (12, 6) (12, 6) (4, 8)

Page 96
1. 12 posters
2. 7 models
3. 10 pages
4. 93, 95, 99
5. 8 shells
6. (2, 2)
7. 34 stamps
8. 2 x 7 < 7 x 3; Jay has more quarters.

Page 97
1. d
2. a
3. d
4. a
5. b
6. b
7. c
8. a
9. c and d
10. d
11. b

Page 98
1. d
2. d
3. c
4. a
5. b
6. d
7. a
8. d
9. b
10. c

Page 100
1. The Comets
2. Red Boas and The Stars
3. 25
4. The Tribe and White Lightning
5. Blue Tornadoes and Red Boas
6. 40
7. Green Sox
8. 35

Page 101
1. candy bars
2. gum
3. five
4. four
5. two
6. mints, kisses, candy bars

Page 102
1. twice
2. half
3. decreased
4. increase
5. both
6. more than
7. total
8. equal
9. in all
10. greater

Page 103
1. no
2. 1996
3. 1997
4. 300
5. yes; 1992 and 1994
6. 1995
7. 500
8. 450 all together
9. 300 fewer
10. 200 more

Page 104
1. certain
2. impossible
3. impossible
4. impossible
5. certain
6. impossible
7. impossible
8. impossible
9. certain
10. certain

Page 106
1. more
2. equally
3. equally
4. less
5. more
6. more
7. more
8. equally
9. less
10. equally

Page 108
1. $25.00
2. 92 degrees
3. They started at 4:00 and took the first break at 4:15.
4. 29 cards
5. 10 fans
6. $25.00

Page 109

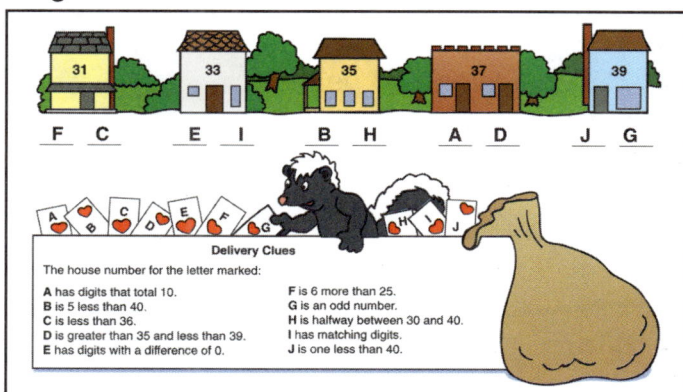

Page 110

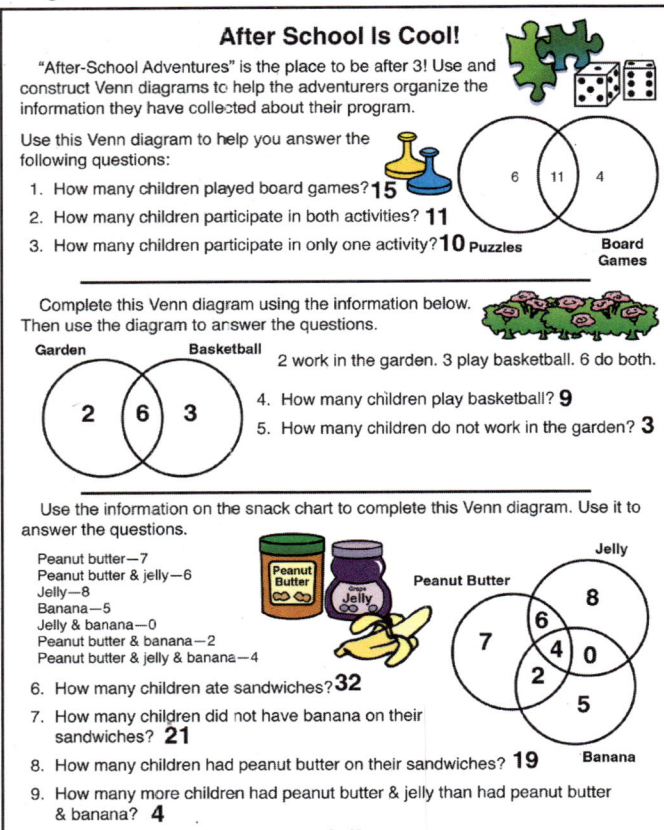

Page 111
1. Colby's favorite topping: Honey and walnuts
2. Lacie's favorite topping: Maple syrup
3. Judson's favorite topping: Chocolate-hazelnut spread
4. Kari's favorite topping: Apple butter
5. Dev's favorite topping: Strawberries and bananas

Page 112
1. 150 pounds
2. 15 people
3. 180 pounds
4. 2.5 miles
5. 77 beats
6. 28 muffins

Page 113
1. sneakers, sandals; sneakers, slippers; sneakers, socks; sneakers, ski boots; sandals, slippers; sandals, socks; sandals, ski boots; slippers, socks; slippers, ski boots; socks, ski boots
2. 1 blue, 1 red, 1 yellow, 2 blue, 2 red, 2 yellow, 3 blue, 3 red, 3 yellow
3. hammerhead, baby, teeth; hammerhead, baby, no teeth; hammerhead, adult, teeth; hammerhead, adult, no teeth; nurse, baby, teeth; nurse, baby, no teeth; nurse, adult, teeth; nurse, adult, no teeth; tiger, baby, teeth; tiger, baby, no teeth; tiger, adult, teeth; tiger, adult, no teeth
4. brown, small; brown, medium; brown, large; white, small; white, medium; white, large
5. strawberry, thick, one, regular; strawberry, thick, two, regular; strawberry, thin, one, regular; strawberry, thin, two, regular; shortcake, thick, one, regular; shortcake, thick, two, regular; shortcake, thin, one, regular; shortcake, thin, two, regular; strawberry, thick, one, jumbo; strawberry, thick, two, jumbo; strawberry, thin, one, jumbo; strawberry, thin, two, jumbo; shortcake, thick, one, jumbo; shortcake, thick, two, jumbo; shortcake, thin, one, jumbo; shortcake, thin, two, jumbo

Page 114
1. 8 marbles, 5 shells
2. 4 quarters, two dimes, and one nickel
   Can also be half dollar, quarter, 5 dimes
3. 14 mints
4. 11 peanuts and 13 peanuts
5. 5 acorns and 15 feathers

Page 115
1. 21¢
2. 42¢
3. 5¢
4. 56¢
5. 24¢
6. 6 squash
7. 8 nickels
8. 5 carrots
9. 5 strawberries in each basket
10. 24¢